DK

RAPPING UP BIOLOGY

with
Matt Green

THE
RAPPING SCIENCE TEACHER

From the author:

To my incredible wife, Helen – there would be no science raps without you. Thank you for being my constant encourager, for believing in me from the very beginning, and for giving me that first push to step in front of the camera. You are, and always have been, my number one supporter. Huge thanks to my mum and dad for instilling in me the value of education and shaping my path to becoming a teacher, and to my wonderful in-laws, Emma and Mike, for your unwavering support. My heartfelt gratitude goes to my management, Wendy Woolfson Talent and PR, for creating this incredible publishing opportunity. Wendy and Hannah – your inspiring work and guidance turn my dreams into reality.
Finally, thank you to DK for believing in this project and bringing it to life.

Author Matt Green, The Rapping Science Teacher
Author Contributors Mark Levesley and Jo Locke

Produced for DK by
Editorial Just Content Limited
Design Fourth Wall

Senior Editor Amelia Jones
Managing Editor Katherine Neep
Managing Art Editors Sarah Corcoran, Elizabeth Arnoux
Pre-Production Designer Rohit Singh
Senior Production Controller Meskerem Berhane
Publisher Sarah Forbes
Managing Director, Learning Hilary Fine

First published in Great Britain in 2026 by
Dorling Kindersley Limited
20 Vauxhall Bridge Road,
London SW1V 2SA

The authorised representative in the EEA is
Dorling Kindersley Verlag GmbH. Arnulfstr. 124,
80636 Munich, Germany

Lyrics copyright © Matt Green 2026
Matt Green has asserted his right to be identified as the author of the lyrics in this work
Text and design copyright © 2026 Dorling Kindersley Limited
A Penguin Random House Company
10 9 8 7 6 5 4 3 2 1
001–352646–Jan/2026

All rights reserved.
No part of this publication may be reproduced, stored in or introduced into a retrieval system, or transmitted, in any form, or by any means (electronic, mechanical, photocopying, recording, or otherwise), without the prior written permission of the copyright owner. DK values and supports copyright. Thank you for respecting intellectual property laws by not reproducing, scanning or distributing any part of this publication by any means without permission. By purchasing an authorised edition, you are supporting writers and artists and enabling DK to continue to publish books that inform and inspire readers. No part of this publication may be used or reproduced in any manner for the purpose of training artificial intelligence technologies or systems. In accordance with Article 4(3) of the DSM Directive 2019/790, DK expressly reserves this work from the text and data mining exception.

A CIP catalogue record for this book is available from the British Library.
ISBN: 978-0-2417-7156-3

Printed and bound in China

www.dk.com

This book was made with Forest Stewardship Council™ certified paper – one small step in DK's commitment to a sustainable future.
Learn more at www.dk.com/uk/ information/sustainability

Welcome from Matt

Welcome to Rapping Up Biology – by me, Matt Green The Rapping Science Teacher!

This book takes everything I've learnt from all my years of teaching in schools and on social media and lays it out in an easy-to-use revision format.

Helping students to understand science means a huge amount to me, so I have put blood, sweat and tears into this guide to make Biology revision not just simple, but unforgettable.

First, read each topic section to understand the key ideas. Then move to the RAPPING UP! section to lock it in with a short, punchy rap that makes the facts stick.

Forget boring textbooks – this guide is your secret weapon, designed to help you master GCSE Biology and walk into your exams with total confidence.

Let's drop the beat and start learning.
Rap. Revise. Remember!

Contents

Cell Biology — 5
- Cells and Microscopy 6
- Prokaryotic Cells 8
- Mitosis and Differentiation 10
- Stem Cells and Cell Specialisation 12
- Diffusion, Osmosis and Active Transport 14
- Factors Affecting Diffusion 16
- Brain Booster 18

Organisation — 19
- Animal Tissues, Organs and Organ Systems 20
- Food Tests 22
- Digestion 24
- Enzyme Action 26
- Circulatory System 28
- Heart Structure 30
- Diseases, Risk Factors and Cancer 32
- Plant Tissues, Organs and Systems 34
- Factors Affecting Transpiration 36
- Brain Booster 38

Infection and Response — 39
- Pathogens 40
- Viral Pathogens 42
- Human Defence Systems 44
- Antibiotics and Drug Development 46
- Plant Diseases and Defences 48
- Brain Booster 50

Bioenergetics — 51
- Photosynthesis 52
- Rate of Photosynthesis 54
- Respiration, Exercise and Metabolism 56
- Brain Booster 58

Homeostasis and Response — 59
- Homeostasis and the Nervous System 60
- The Brain and Temperature Control 62
- The Eye 64
- The Endocrine System 66
- Control of Blood Glucose 68
- Water Balance 70
- Reproductive Hormones 72
- Contraception 74
- Plant Hormones 76
- Brain Booster 78

Inheritance, Variation and Evolution — 79
- Asexual and Sexual Reproduction 80
- DNA 82
- Genetic Inheritance 84
- Effects of Genes 86
- Variation and Classification 88
- Evolution 90
- Theories of Evolution 91
- Evidence for Evolution 92
- Genetic Engineering and Cloning 94
- Brain Booster 96

Ecology — 97
- Communities 98
- Ecosystems Organisation and Energy Transfer 100
- Natural Cycles 102
- Human Impacts on Biodiversity 104
- Food Security 106
- Brain Booster 108

Answers 109
Exam Board References 111
Acknowledgments 112

Cell Biology

At the end of this chapter, you should be able to:

- ✓ Explain how microscopes are used.
- ✓ Label cell organelles on diagrams of different cells and describe what each organelle does.
- ✓ Compare different cell types.
- ✓ Describe how cells make copies of themselves.
- ✓ Describe how cells become specialised and identify features that help these cells do their jobs.
- ✓ Explain the benefits and risks of using stem cells.
- ✓ Explain how substances enter and leave cells.
- ✓ Explain how the speed of diffusion can change.

Cell Biology

Cells and Microscopy

Key terms

- Cell membrane
- Cell wall
- Chloroplast
- Cytoplasm
- Eukaryotic cell
- Mitochondrion
- Nucleus
- Organelle
- Ribosome
- Vacuole

Plant and animal cells are **eukaryotic** cells. All eukaryotic cells have a nucleus and other subcellular organelles.

Science skills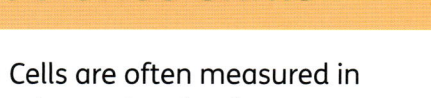

- Cells are often measured in micrometres (µm).

  1 m = 1000 mm and 1 mm = 1000 µm

- Estimation – a rough calculation.

To estimate the area of a plant cell, imagine it is a rectangle:
10 µm × 30 µm = 300 µm²

To estimate the size of a nucleus, imagine how many will fit along the longer side of the cell: about 7, so 30 µm ÷ 7 is approximately 4 µm.

Animal cell

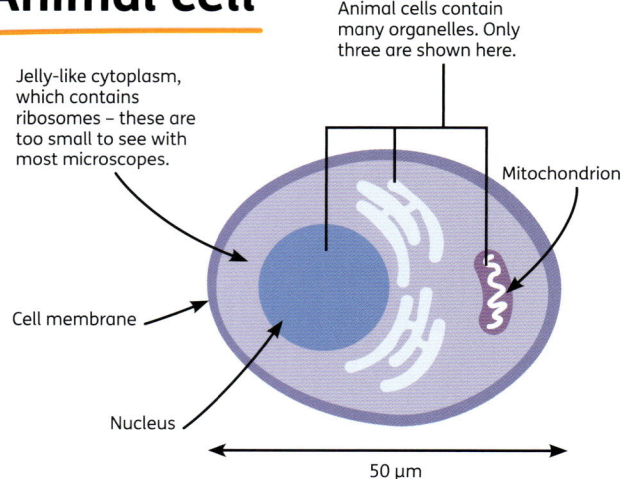

Animal cells contain many organelles. Only three are shown here.

Jelly-like cytoplasm, which contains ribosomes – these are too small to see with most microscopes.

Cell membrane

Nucleus

Mitochondrion

50 µm

Plant cell

Microscopes show a 2D flat slice through a cell, but remember that cells are 3D objects, as this diagram shows.

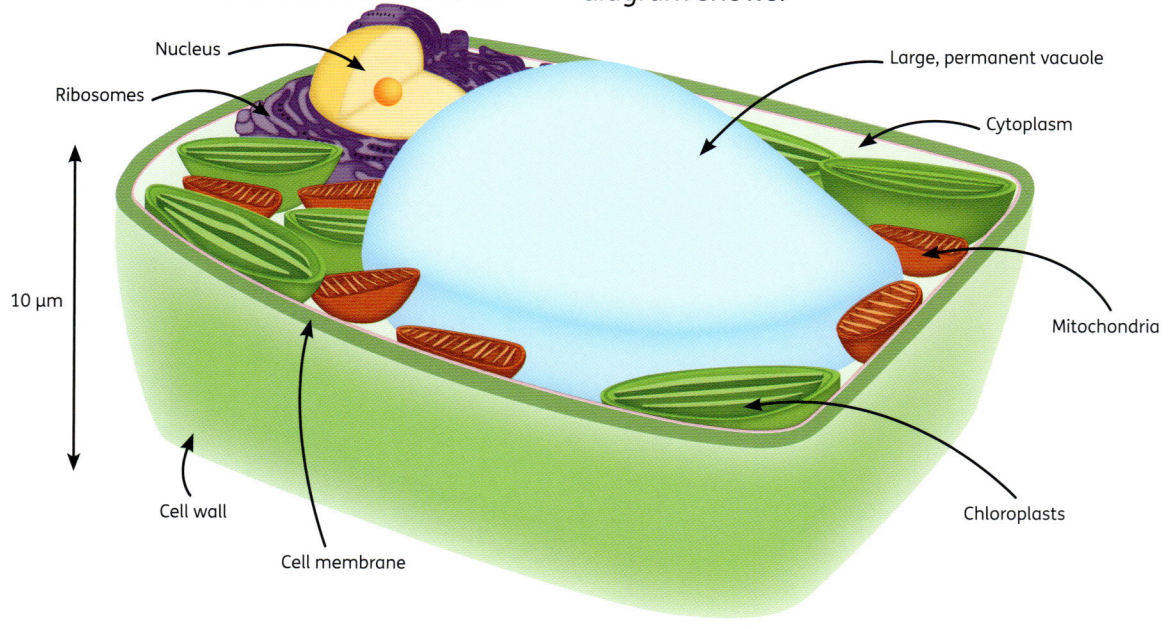

Nucleus, Ribosomes, Cell wall, Cell membrane, Large permanent vacuole, Cytoplasm, Mitochondria, Chloroplasts

10 µm

30 µm

Cell Biology

Microscopes

With time, microscopes have developed greater:

- Magnifying power (the number of times bigger specimens appear).
- Resolving power (the ability to show neighbouring objects as two separate objects).

Light microscopes use light to see specimens, but newer electron microscopes use streams of electrons. They are more powerful and resolve things in very fine detail. However, electron microscopes are very big and cannot be used to examine living cells.

The developments in microscopes have greatly increased our knowledge of cell structure and functioning.

Science skills

To calculate total magnification:

Total microscope magnification = eyepiece lens power × objective lens power

To calculate the real size of an object:

Real size of an object =

$$\frac{\text{Image size seen under microscope}}{\text{Total magnification}}$$

A light microscope

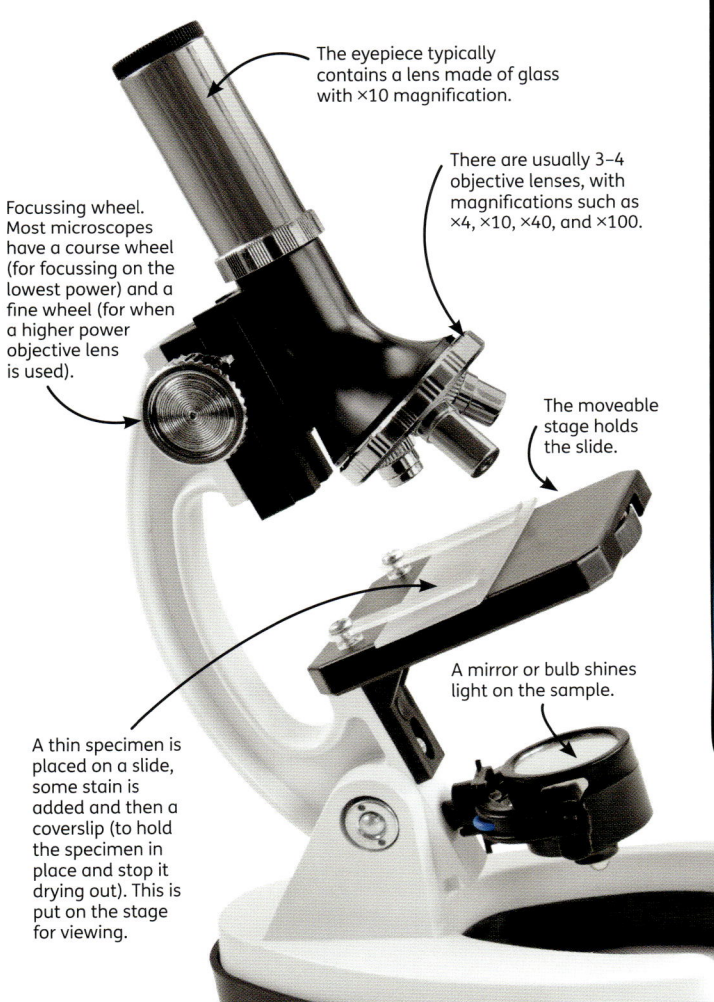

- The eyepiece typically contains a lens made of glass with ×10 magnification.
- There are usually 3–4 objective lenses, with magnifications such as ×4, ×10, ×40, and ×100.
- Focussing wheel. Most microscopes have a course wheel (for focussing on the lowest power) and a fine wheel (for when a higher power objective lens is used).
- The moveable stage holds the slide.
- A mirror or bulb shines light on the sample.
- A thin specimen is placed on a slide, some stain is added and then a coverslip (to hold the specimen in place and stop it drying out). This is put on the stage for viewing.

RAPPING UP!

I'm teaching you cells, now let me cook.
Pick up the microscope, now we look.
Learning all of these structures is easy.
Starting with middle is the **nucleus**.

That's the part that makes things happen.
Cytoplasm – chemical reactions.
Cell membrane - it goes all around,
controls what comes in and comes out.

Now, **Mi-to-con-dria**.
Energy release happens here.
Ribosomes are near,
they make proteins all year.

Animals done, next thing is hard.
Cell wall, **vacuole**, chloroplasts.
Those three there are specific to plants.
Photosynthesis is the heart.

Takes in light and CO_2.
Combines to water then makes food.
Chlorophyll is where this brews.
Along with glucose comes O_2.

Cell Biology

Prokaryotic Cells

Key terms

- Aseptic technique
- Binary fission
- Colony
- Order of magnitude
- Prokaryotic cell
- Plasmid

Prokaryotic cells are smaller than eukaryotic cells and do not have large organelles. Their genetic material is not inside a complex nucleus – it's just a single DNA loop in the cytoplasm. There may also be other small rings of DNA called **plasmids**. Bacteria are prokaryotic.

A typical bacterium

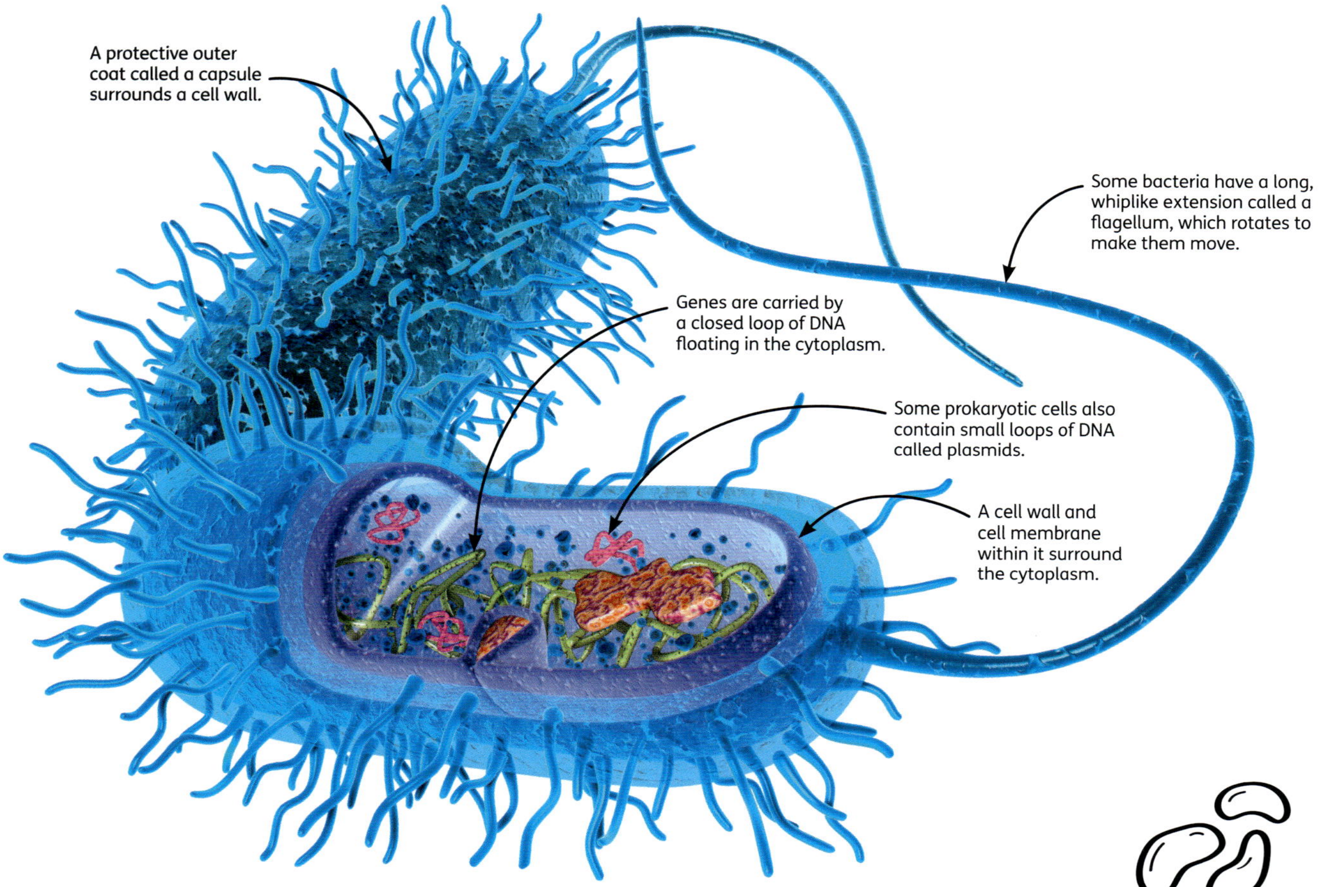

- A protective outer coat called a capsule surrounds a cell wall.
- Some bacteria have a long, whiplike extension called a flagellum, which rotates to make them move.
- Genes are carried by a closed loop of DNA floating in the cytoplasm.
- Some prokaryotic cells also contain small loops of DNA called plasmids.
- A cell wall and cell membrane within it surround the cytoplasm.

Bacterial growth

Bacteria reproduce by dividing in two. This is **binary fission**. If they have enough nutrients and a warm temperature, a bacterial cell can divide every 20 minutes. In school science labs, bacteria are incubated at 25°C, since temperatures higher than this can cause dangerous pathogens to grow.

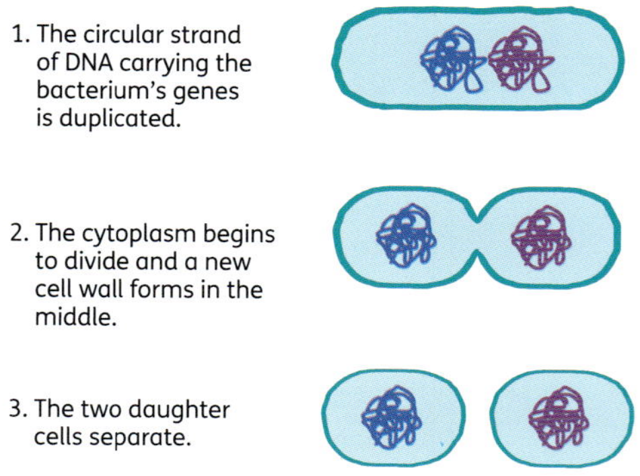

1. The circular strand of DNA carrying the bacterium's genes is duplicated.

2. The cytoplasm begins to divide and a new cell wall forms in the middle.

3. The two daughter cells separate.

Cell Biology

Science skills

Bacterial division time is how long it takes a daughter cell to grow and then divide. You can use this to estimate the number of bacteria present.

Calculate the number of divisions $n = \dfrac{\text{Time period}}{\text{Division time}}$

Number of bacteria at end of the time period = Number of bacteria at start $\times 2^n$

For example, in 10 hours (600 minutes), with a division time of 40 minutes:

	Population A – 1 bacterium	Population B – 250 bacteria
	$n = \dfrac{600}{40} = 15$	$n = \dfrac{600}{40} = 15$
	1×2^{15} $= 1 \times (2 \times 2 \times 2 \times 2 \times 2 \times 2 \times 2 \times 2 \times 2 \times 2 \times 2 \times 2 \times 2 \times 2 \times 2)$ $= 32{,}768$	250×2^{15} $= 8{,}192{,}000$
In standard form (2 significant figures)	3.3×10^4	8.2×10^6

A nutrient broth is a solution containing all the nutrients bacteria need to grow such as sugars, amino acids, vitamins and minerals. If it is heated with agar, it turns into a jelly and can be poured into Petri dishes to set.

When grown on agar jelly "plates", bacterial colonies (billions of cells) appear as blobs. If you spread bacteria all over the plate to grow, and then add discs containing antibiotics, antiseptics or disinfectants, you can see how effectively they kill bacteria (see pages 46–47).

An agar plate

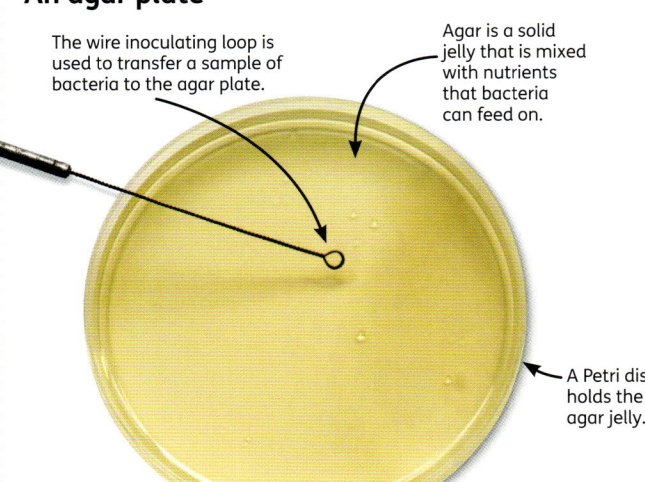

The wire inoculating loop is used to transfer a sample of bacteria to the agar plate.

Agar is a solid jelly that is mixed with nutrients that bacteria can feed on.

A Petri dish holds the agar jelly.

When growing and transferring bacteria, use **aseptic technique**. This stops other microorganisms growing, avoiding contamination. Techniques include:

- Sterilising apparatus and broth in an autoclave.
- Sterilising inoculating loops in a Bunsen flame before each use.
- Plates and broth containers being opened as little as possible.
- Sealing Petri dishes with strips of tape to allow some air in and out, but not microorganisms.

Plates should also be stored upside down so that condensation does not drip onto the agar and spread out the bacteria.

Aseptic technique

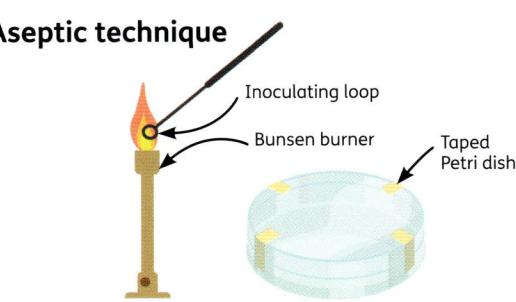

Inoculating loop
Bunsen burner
Taped Petri dish

Cell Biology

Mitosis and Differentiation

Key terms

- Cell cycle
- Cell division
- Differentiation
- Diploid
- Meristem
- Mitosis
- Specialised cell

Cell division is when cells make identical copies of themselves. It occurs during the cell cycle.

Importance of cell division

- Growth and development of multicellular organisms (made of many cells).
- Repair of organs and tissues.
- Asexual reproduction (see pages 80–81).

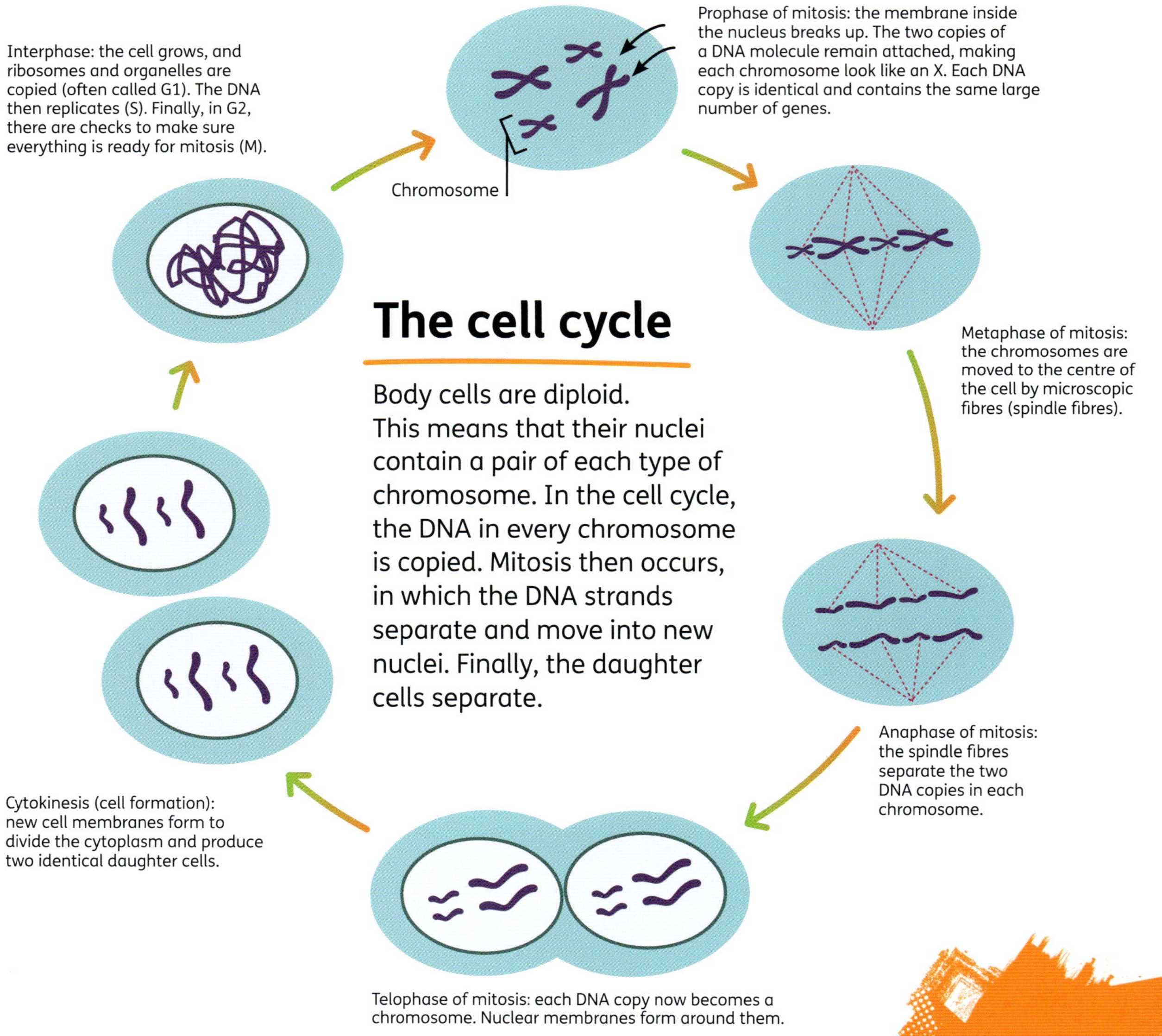

Interphase: the cell grows, and ribosomes and organelles are copied (often called G1). The DNA then replicates (S). Finally, in G2, there are checks to make sure everything is ready for mitosis (M).

Prophase of mitosis: the membrane inside the nucleus breaks up. The two copies of a DNA molecule remain attached, making each chromosome look like an X. Each DNA copy is identical and contains the same large number of genes.

Chromosome

Metaphase of mitosis: the chromosomes are moved to the centre of the cell by microscopic fibres (spindle fibres).

The cell cycle

Body cells are diploid. This means that their nuclei contain a pair of each type of chromosome. In the cell cycle, the DNA in every chromosome is copied. Mitosis then occurs, in which the DNA strands separate and move into new nuclei. Finally, the daughter cells separate.

Anaphase of mitosis: the spindle fibres separate the two DNA copies in each chromosome.

Cytokinesis (cell formation): new cell membranes form to divide the cytoplasm and produce two identical daughter cells.

Telophase of mitosis: each DNA copy now becomes a chromosome. Nuclear membranes form around them.

Cell Biology

Cell differentiation

Some cells develop new shapes and cell structures to carry out specific functions. They become specialised cells, for example, muscle cells. This development process is differentiation.

Differentiation allows multicellular organisms to have complex tissues and organs that perform specialised functions efficiently.

RAPPING UP!

Mitosis. It's a process
when cells divide. If you notice,
for repair. And what growth is.
Starts in the **nucleus** – that's the hostess.

Replication chromosomes split,
line up in the middle of the cell all **focused**.
Then pull apart to the opposite sides.
Chromatids here. Now the cell divides
when the cell splits itself into two pieces.

That moment right there is called **cytokinesis**.
What you now have is two daughter cells.
With identical chromosome numbers as well.

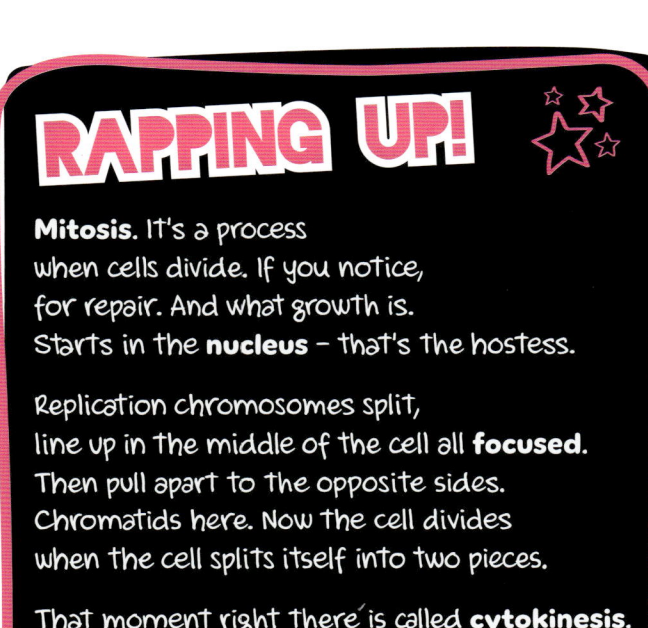

Meristems

Most animal cells can only differentiate very early in life, but cells in plant meristems can differentiate throughout a plant's life. Meristem cells divide rapidly, and the daughter cells then differentiate into root hair cells, xylem cells, palisade cells – in fact, any type of plant cell!

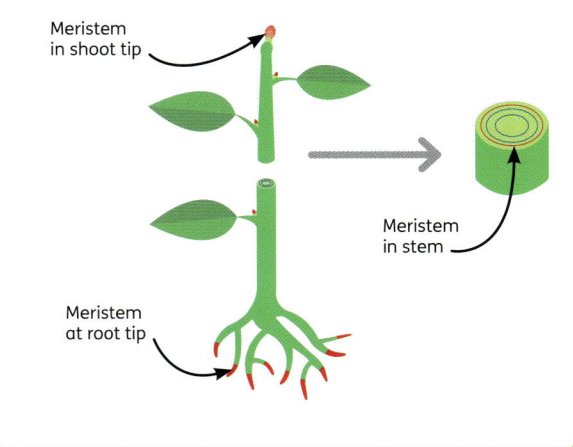

Meristem in shoot tip
Meristem in stem
Meristem at root tip

Cuttings

Meristems are the reason why cuttings can develop into new plants.

Cuttings grow new roots from meristem tissue in the stem.

Cell Biology

Stem Cells and Cell Specialisation

Key terms

- Adult stem cells
- Embryonic stem cells
- Stem cells
- Therapeutic cloning

Cells that have differentiated are specialised for their functions. There are many types.

Examples of specialised cells in animals

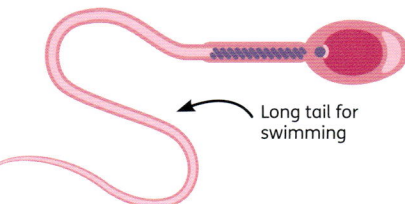

Sperm cells are produced by male animals. They use their long tail to swim through body fluids to reach female sex cells (eggs).

Long tail for swimming

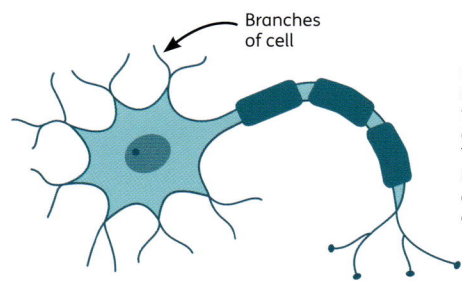

Nerve cells are specialised to conduct electrical signals. They have tiny branches to connect with other nerve cells.

Branches of cell

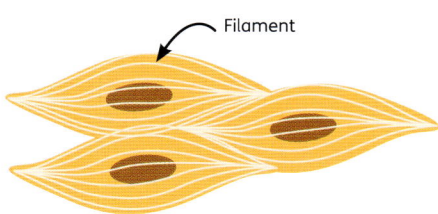

Muscle cells have filaments that interweave, allowing the cells to contract rapidly and so produce muscle movement.

Filament

RAPPING UP!

Does one job – **that's a** specialised cell.
Start with **sperm** coz it's got a long tail
swims like hell over to the female
to fuse with an egg and make a boy or a girl.

Muscle cells contract and relax;
to the bones of the skeleton they attach.
Glygogen inside – that's a fact.
Gotta go gym if you wanna get stacked.

Nerve cells – that's the mood I'm in –
stretch through your body like string.
Axons covered in **myelin**:
they're in your toes and in your chin.

Root hair cells they take in water;
xylem cells are the transporter
of the water, up the plant.
They work in full – no halves or quarters.

Phloem cells? Little bit shorter –
move things in a different order:
up and down and only food,
inside the stem and not the border.

Examples of specialised cells in plants

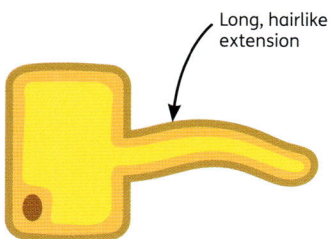

Long, hairlike extension

Root hair cells have long, hairlike extensions that absorb water and minerals from the soil.

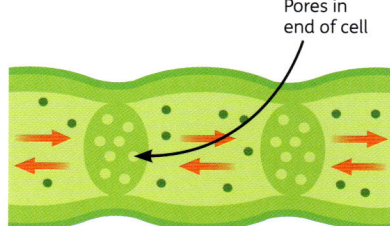

Pores in end of cell

Phloem cells transport sugar around the plant. These tube-like cells have porous walls that are joined end-to-end.

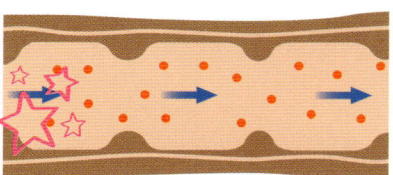

Xylem cells carry water up from a plant's roots to its leaves. The cells have open ends that join together to form a tube.

Cell Biology

Stem cells

Stem cells are undifferentiated cells that divide to produce cells that can then differentiate. Plant stem cells are found in meristems. In animals, there are two types:

- Cells produced by **embryonic stem cells** – these can differentiate into any type of cell.
- Cells from **adult stem cells** – these can only differentiate into some types of specialised cell.

Adult stem cells

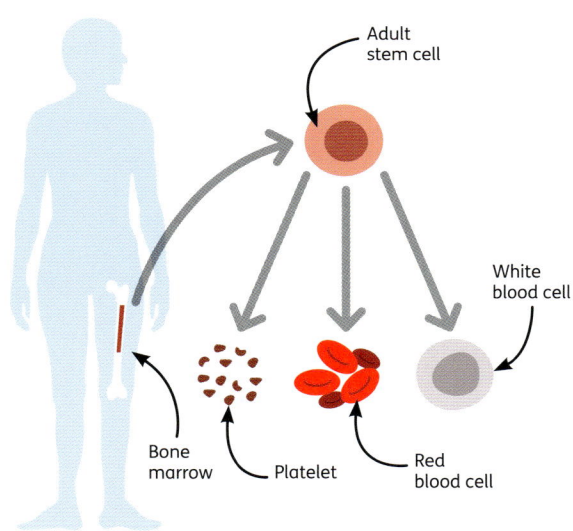

Embryonic stem cells

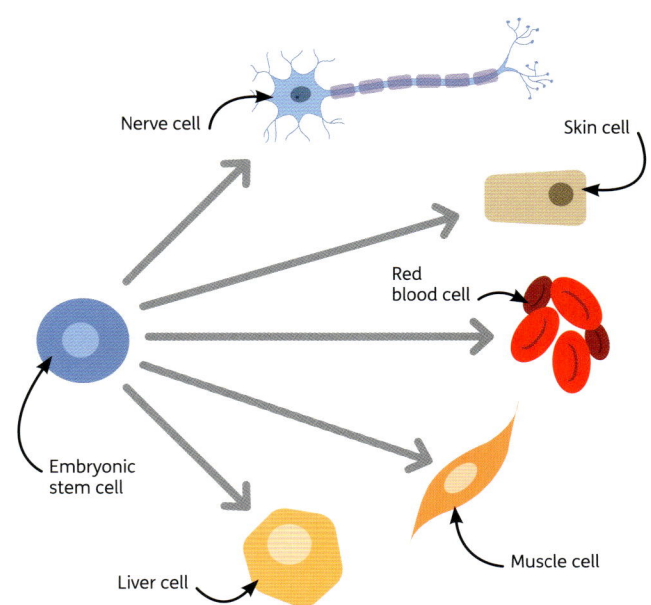

There are different types of animal stem cell, found in different parts of the body.
For example, the adult stem cells that produce blood cells are found in bone marrow.

Potential stem cell uses

Adult stem cells are being trialled to produce:

- Nerve cells to repair spinal cord damage to treat paralysis.
- Insulin-producing cells in the pancreas to treat diabetes.

Treatments are also being developed using embryonic stem cells made from a patient's own cells by adult cell cloning. Embryonic stem cells made by this therapeutic cloning technique contain the same DNA as all the other cells in the patient, and so are not rejected (attacked by the immune system) (see pages 94–95).

Stem cell treatment problems

- Viruses may infect stem cells grown in a lab (and therefore get into a patient).
- Some people think it is wrong to use and destroy human embryos.

Meristem uses

- Farmers use clones (identical copies) of crop plants with useful features such as disease resistance.
- Meristem tissue is used to produce thousands of clones of a plant quickly and cheaply using "tissue culture".
- Cloning a rare species in this way can also save it from extinction (see pages 94–95).

Cell Biology

Diffusion, Osmosis and Active Transport

Key terms

- Active transport
- Concentration gradient
- Diffusion
- Osmosis
- Partially permeable membrane

Key facts

- Particles in gases and liquids are constantly moving in all directions.
- There are so many particles in regions of higher concentration that vast numbers are moving from the higher to lower concentration. There are, of course, some that are moving in the opposite direction.
- This produces a net (overall) movement of particles down the **concentration gradient** from higher to lower.
- This net movement is diffusion.

Osmosis

Osmosis is the diffusion of water particles through a **partially permeable membrane**.

There is a net movement of water molecules from their higher concentration (a dilute solution of solute) to their lower concentration (a concentrated solution of solute).

Substances can move into and out of cells by **diffusion, osmosis** and **active transport**.

Diffusion

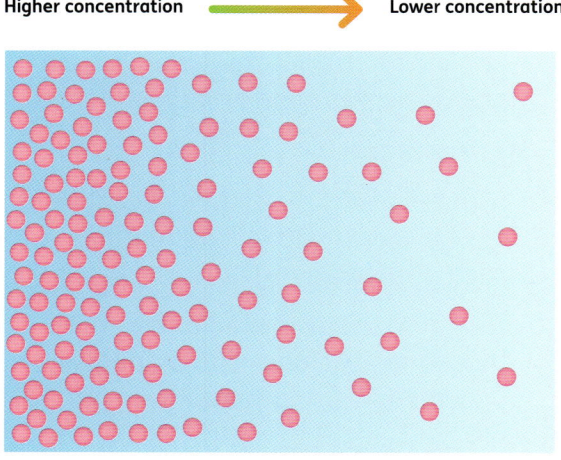

Diffusion vs. Osmosis

Diffusion Net movement of solute particles.

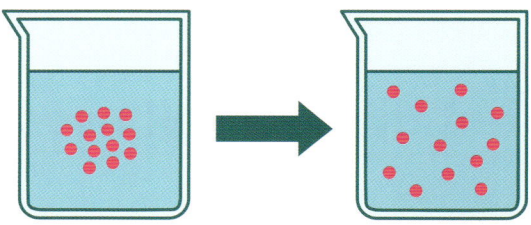

Osmosis Net movement of water particles through a partially permeable membrane.

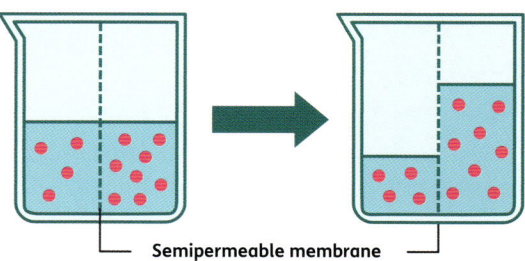

A partially permeable membrane has tiny pores in it, through which water molecules can fit, but not larger solute molecules.

Cell Biology

Science skills

1. Take five different concentrations of sucrose solution.
2. Put 15 potato tissue cylinders into five groups of three.
3. Measure the mass of each group.
4. Add each group to a different beaker and leave for an hour.
5. Remove the cylinders and pat them dry with a paper towel.
6. Measure the mass of each group again.
7. Calculate the water uptake for each group (in g/min). A negative value is a loss of water.
8. Calculate the percentage change in mass for each group.

Results

Table of results	A	B	C	D	E
Sugar concentration (mol dm^{-3})	0.2	0.4	0.6	0.8	1.0
Percentage change in mass	10	0	−5	−15	−20

↰ A percentage change accounts for the fact that the cylinders start with different initial masses.

$$\text{Percentage change in mass} = \frac{\text{Final mass} - \text{Original mass}}{\text{Original mass}} \times 100$$

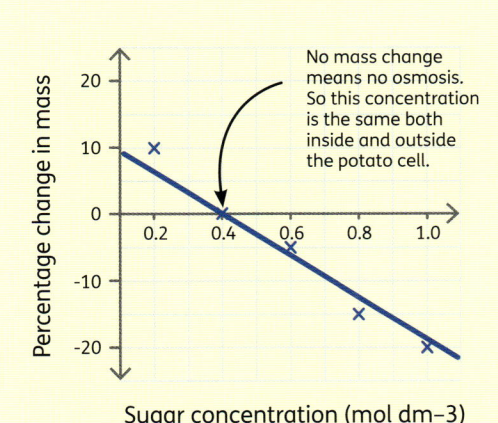

No mass change means no osmosis. So this concentration is the same both inside and outside the potato cell.

Active transport

Active transport uses tiny pumps in cell membranes to move substances against their concentration gradients. For example:

- Mineral ions (for healthy plant growth) are pumped into plant root hair cells from very dilute solutions in the soil.
- A while after a meal, sugar concentration in the blood is higher than in the small intestine. To get all the sugars from the meal they must be pumped into the blood.

The membrane pumps need energy from respiration. Diffusion and osmosis do not require energy.

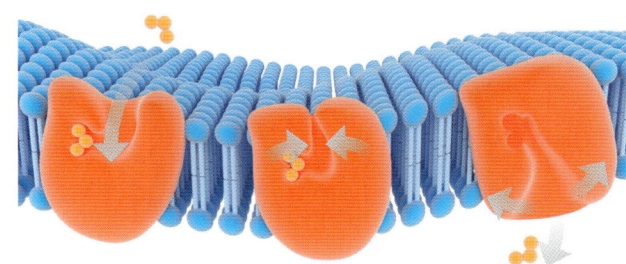

Membrane pumps

RAPPING UP!

Time I clear up confusion.
I'll do **osmosis** and **diffusion**.
Repeat what I say – no excusing;
repeat what I say – you're improving.

Concentration **high to low**;
concentration high to low.
Only difference is osmosis
just does this for H₂O.

But that's through a membrane though,
so the **solutes cannot go**.
More solutes inside the cell
means inside the water flows.

Active transport so you know
does not move things high to low;
it moves things from **low to high**
and that is just how it goes.

Cell Biology

Factors Affecting Diffusion

Key terms

- Alveolus
- Bronchus
- Gas exchange
- Surface area to volume ratio (SA:V)
- Trachea

Diffusion allows cells to obtain important substances, such as oxygen, and lose waste (for example, urea and carbon dioxide). Three main factors affect the rate of diffusion.

Factor	Diffusion rate is increased by	Explanation
Concentration gradient	Greater difference between concentrations	The more particles in the higher concentration region, the more particles there are to move to the lower concentration region.
Temperature	Higher temperature	Particles move faster at higher temperatures.
Surface area	Greater area	There is more area through which particles can move.

Surface area to volume ratios

A cell needs a large surface area for substances to diffuse into it and quickly fill all its volume. It needs a large **surface area to volume ratio (SA:V ratio)**. A single-celled organism has a high SA:V ratio, allowing enough molecules to enter and leave by diffusion to survive.

The SA:V ratio is calculated by dividing surface area by volume.

Transport systems

Multicellular organisms have very small SA:V ratios. Therefore, they need exchange surfaces through which substances can pass efficiently. These surfaces are linked to transport systems (for example, the circulatory system), which take substances to and from all their cells.

Exchange surfaces are efficient when they have:

- A large surface area.
- A thin membrane (so that substances do not have to diffuse far).
- A good supply of blood (in animals).
- Good ventilation (exchange of the fluid containing oxygen in animals).

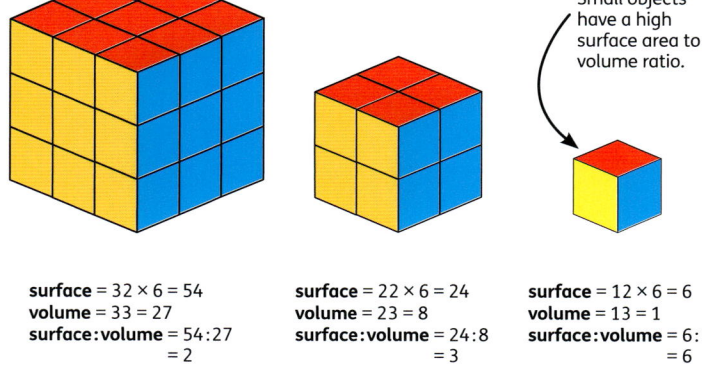

Small objects have a high surface area to volume ratio.

surface = $3^2 \times 6 = 54$
volume = $3^3 = 27$
surface:volume = $54:27$
= 2

surface = $2^2 \times 6 = 24$
volume = $2^3 = 8$
surface:volume = $24:8$
= 3

surface = $1^2 \times 6 = 6$
volume = $1^3 = 1$
surface:volume = $6:1$
= 6

Cell Biology

Examples of exchange surfaces

Lungs
The exchange surfaces in the lungs are well adapted for efficient **gas exchange**.

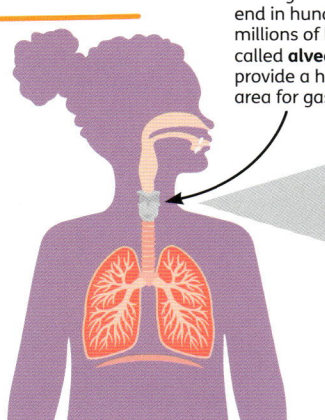

The **trachea** divides into two **bronchi**, one going to each lung. Inside the lungs, the air tubes get smaller and end in hundreds of millions of little sacs, called **alveoli**. These provide a huge surface area for gas exchange.

Good ventilation changes the air frequently, removing carbon dioxide and supplying oxygen.

Deoxygenated blood arrives from the heart.

Carbon dioxide diffuses into the alveolus from the blood.

Oxygenated blood flows back to the heart.

Oxygen from the alveolus diffuses into the blood.

The wall of an alveolus is only one cell thick.

Alveoli are covered in a network of blood capillaries. The capillary walls are only one cell thick.

Gas exchange within an alveolus

Small intestine
The small intestine has thin walls, and its surface area is increased by being very long and having **villi**.

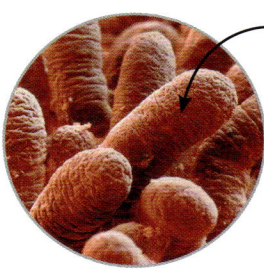

Thousands of projections called villi give the intestine a large surface area.

Gills
Fish pump water through their gills, helped by opening and closing their mouths. This ventilates the gills.

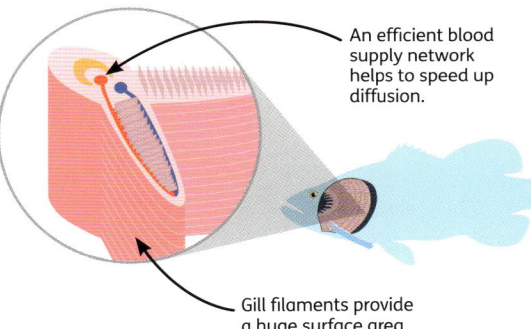

An efficient blood supply network helps to speed up diffusion.

Gill filaments provide a huge surface area.

Plant exchange surfaces

- Root surface area is increased by root hairs.
- Leaves have stomata for gas exchange and are thin so gases do not have to travel far between the outside and the cells inside the leaf.

RAPPING UP!

We use these for taking a breath:
oxygen in – I say this with chest.
CO_2? That needs to leave.
Let me explain to you how we breathe.

Air goes straight down through the **windpipe** –
or the trachea if saying it right.
At this point here we see that it splits:
now it's the **bronchi** – it's in two bits.

Raising the surface area's the goal
so they know to branch into bronchioles.
Ending with these – numbers are high,
remember the name – they're the **alveoli**.

Take a look and I will explain:
this is the site of gas exchange.

Oxygen goes through these **membranes**,
flows down from high to low concentra - tion.
Into the blood its gone;
we call that process **diffusion**.
Then by the cells oxygen's consumed;
we call that one respiration.

Carbon dioxide – there's no room –
has to go back to the lungs by noon.
To fill up the space in these balloons
take a breath out – I'll see you soon.

18 Brain Booster

Cell Biology Recap Quiz

 Find a pen and paper and work through these revision questions.

1. Complete the sentence. Each blank is one word.
   _____ is the diffusion of water through a _____ permeable membrane.

2. State **one** feature found in the cytoplasm of a bacterial cell but not in an animal cell.

3. Name a specialised cell in animals used to transmit electrical signals.

4. Give **one** reason why mitosis is important.

5. Explain the effect of temperature on the speed of diffusion.

6. Calculate the SA:V ratio of a cube of side length 2.5 cm.

7. Some microscopes are better at showing two close objects as being separate. What is this feature called? Choose one.
   resolution   focussing   power   magnification

8. State **two** things that happen in a cell before mitosis.

9. Which plant cells transport water? Choose one.
   meristem   xylem   palisade   phloem

10. State **one** substance that plants take into root hair cells using active transport.

11. Explain why inoculating loops are passed through a Bunsen flame before each use.

12. A microscope has a ×5 eyepiece lens and a ×20 objective lens. What is its total magnifying power?

13. State the difference between adult and embryonic stem cells.

14. In which organelle would you find chlorophyll?

15. Why are agar "plates" stored upside down?

Check your answers on page **109**.

Organisation

At the end of this chapter, you should be able to:

- ✓ Explain how the body is organised.
- ✓ Describe how to test foods for the presence of starch, sugar, protein and lipids.
- ✓ Describe the role of bile and enzymes in digestion.
- ✓ Explain enzyme specificity and the factors that affect enzyme action.
- ✓ Describe the structure and function of the circulatory system.
- ✓ Compare treatments for coronary heart disease.
- ✓ Give examples of risk factors that increase the risk of non-communicable diseases.
- ✓ Explain what is meant by cancer.
- ✓ Explain how a leaf is adapted for photosynthesis.
- ✓ Describe how materials are transported around a plant.
- ✓ Describe the factors that affect the rate of transpiration.

Animal Tissues, Organs and Organ Systems

Key terms

- Cell
- Organ
- Organ system
- Organism
- Plasma
- Platelet
- Red blood cell
- Tissue
- White blood cell

Key facts

- **Cells** are the basic building blocks of all living organisms, for example, muscle cells and red blood cells.
- A **tissue** is a group of cells with a similar structure and function, for example, nervous and epithelial tissue.
- An **organ** is made up of a number of tissues working together to perform a specific function. The brain and kidneys are examples.
- Organs are organised into **organ systems**, which work together to form an **organism**. The nervous system and circulatory system are examples.

Blood

Blood is an example of an animal tissue. It is mainly made up of plasma.

Red blood cells, white blood cells and platelets are transported around the body in the plasma.

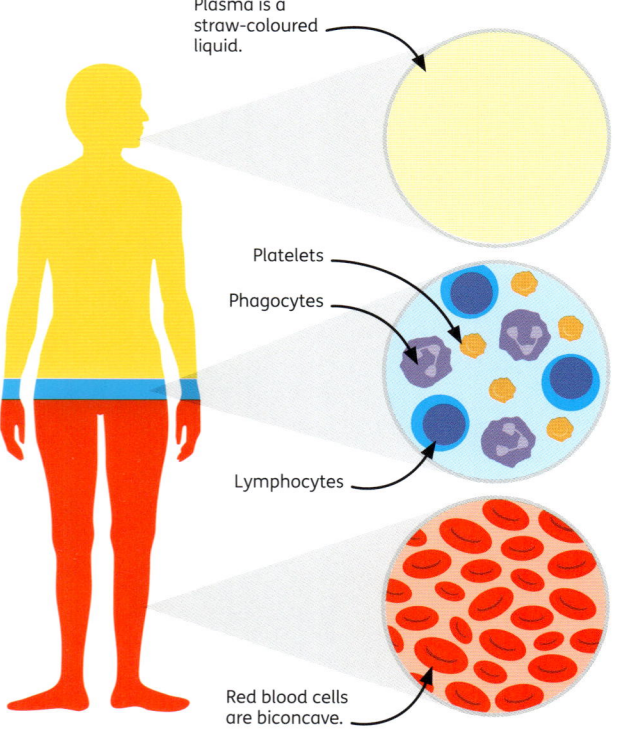

Plasma
Plasma mainly consists of water. Substances including nutrients, waste (carbon dioxide and urea), hormones and antibodies are dissolved in this liquid and transported to all the cells of the body.

White blood cells and platelets
There are two main types of white blood cell – lymphocytes and phagocytes (see page 44). Lymphocytes produce chemicals called antibodies that attack pathogens, while phagocytes engulf and destroy pathogens. White blood cells have a nucleus. Platelets are tiny cell fragments with no nucleus. They clump together to form clots.

Red blood cells (erythrocytes)
Red blood cells are small, flexible discs that can squeeze through blood vessels. They are described as biconcave because each side of the disc has a concave depression. Red blood cells have no nuclei and are packed with haemoglobin, which carries oxygen.

Organisation

RAPPING UP!

Red blood cells – in the bloodstream
White blood cells as well – in the bloodstream
Plasma and the **platelets** dwell – in the bloodstream
And useful matter carried around – in the bloodstream
We're looking at the blood; I'll show you what it does.
It makes its way through the **veins**, then it travels to the lungs.
CO_2's out as waste, and then O_2's in to sub.
Imma show close up to see what it's made of.
When I show this sample, you see the layers **split up** (uh-huh).
When I count **four rows**, there's four things in the blood (yeah).
If I'm starting at the bottom, there's a colour like **rust**:
they're the red blood cells, they're both small and tough.
They carry **haemoglobin** and their shape is like this:
thicker at the edges, it's a **biconcave** disc.
If you watch how they move, you can see they have no **nucleus**;
they pick up **oxygen** so much you'd think they're driving a Prius.

In the tube at the second level, we have protection:
they're the white blood cells and they fight **infections**.
But hold up for one sec, we call this immunity.
The way they fight germs is to drop antibodies.
I'm full focused, bro, the **platelets** come next;
they make the blood clot, in case you never guessed.
Now plasma comes in last place, in case you never know;
it carries all of the above and then it's ready to flow.

Digestive system

The digestive system is an example of an organ system. Many organs work together to digest large, insoluble food molecules into smaller, soluble molecules, which can then be absorbed and used by the body. This process takes place in the digestive system.

Organs in the digestive system

The digestive system consists mainly of a long, muscular tube that squeezes food through the body. It begins at the mouth and ends at the anus.

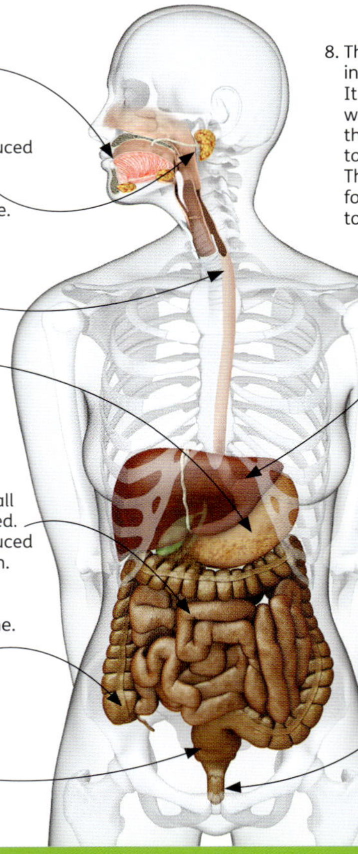

1. Food is broken down in the mouth by chewing. The teeth cut and crush the food into smaller pieces.
2. The food is mixed with saliva produced in the salivary glands. Saliva is a digestive juice – a fluid containing digestive enzymes such as amylase.
3. When you swallow, the oesophagus (a muscular tube) moves food to the stomach.
4. In the stomach, the food is mixed with acid, which kills any microorganisms present in the food and provides the optimum conditions for stomach enzymes to work.
5. Digestive juices from the liver and pancreas are released into the small intestine and digestion is completed. The small, soluble molecules produced are absorbed into the blood stream.
6. Only food that cannot be digested reaches the large intestine. Here, water is absorbed into the bloodstream, leaving a mass of undigested food called faeces.
7. Faeces are stored in the rectum until they leave the body.
8. The liver is also involved in digestion. It produces bile, which it releases into the small intestine to emulsify lipids. This makes it easier for the enzymes to digest them.
9. The anus is a muscular ring through which faeces pass out of the body. This removal of undigested waste is known as egestion.

Organisation

Food Tests

Key terms

- Benedict's solution
- Biuret's solution
- Iodine
- Reagent

Key facts

- Qualitative **reagents** detect whether a nutrient is present in a food, but they do not tell you how much of it is present.
- If a nutrient is present, the reagent changes colour.
- Many foods need to be crushed with a pestle and mortar and dissolved in distilled water to create a solution before testing.

Science skills

If a food contains starch, it will turn blue-black when iodine is added.

- Add a few drops of orange iodine solution.
- Stir the mixture.
- If the solution turns blue-black, it contains iodine.

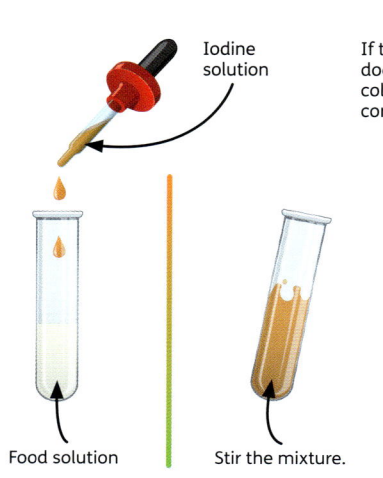 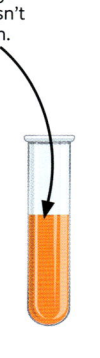 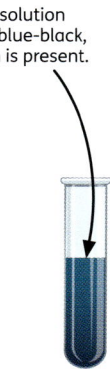

Iodine solution

If the solution doesn't change colour, it doesn't contain starch.

If the solution turns blue-black, starch is present.

Food solution — Stir the mixture.

If a food contains sugar (glucose), it will turn brick red when Benedict's solution is added.

- Add a few drops of bright blue Benedict's solution.
- Stir the mixture and heat in a water bath set at 50°C.
- If the solution turns red, it contains iodine.

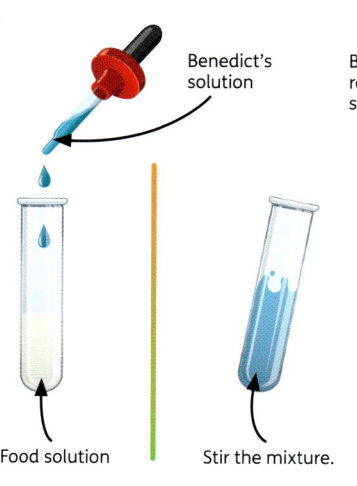 

Benedict's solution

Benedict's solution remains blue if simple sugars are not present.

If the solution contains simple sugars, it will change to a red colour.

Food solution — Stir the mixture.

Organisation

Science skills

If a food contains protein, it will turn purple when Biuret's solution is added.

- Add a few drops of blue Biuret's solution (a mixture of potassium hydroxide and copper sulfate).
- Stir the mixture.
- If the solution turns purple, it contains protein.

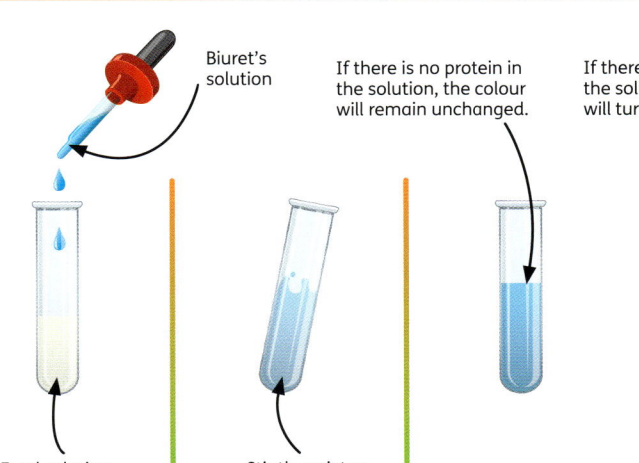

If a food contains lipids, a white emulsion will form when ethanol is added.

- Add a few drops of clear ethanol solution.
- Stir the mixture.
- Pour some of the mixture into a test tube of distilled water.
- If a white emulsion appears, the solution contains lipids.

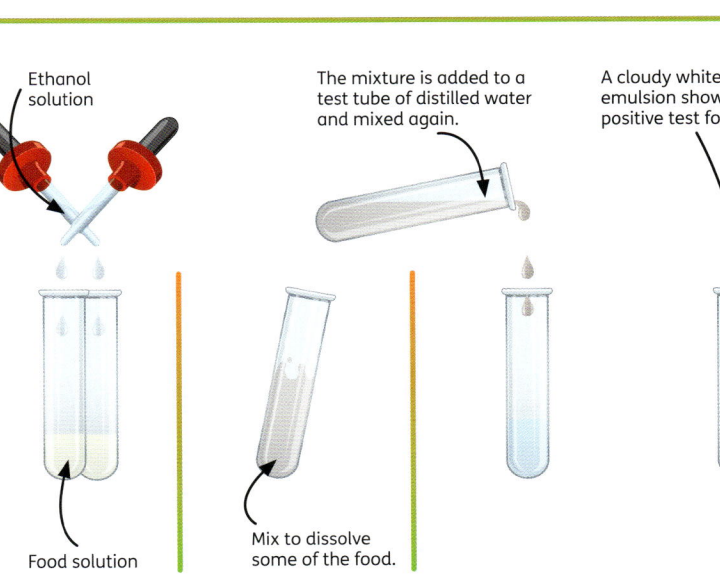

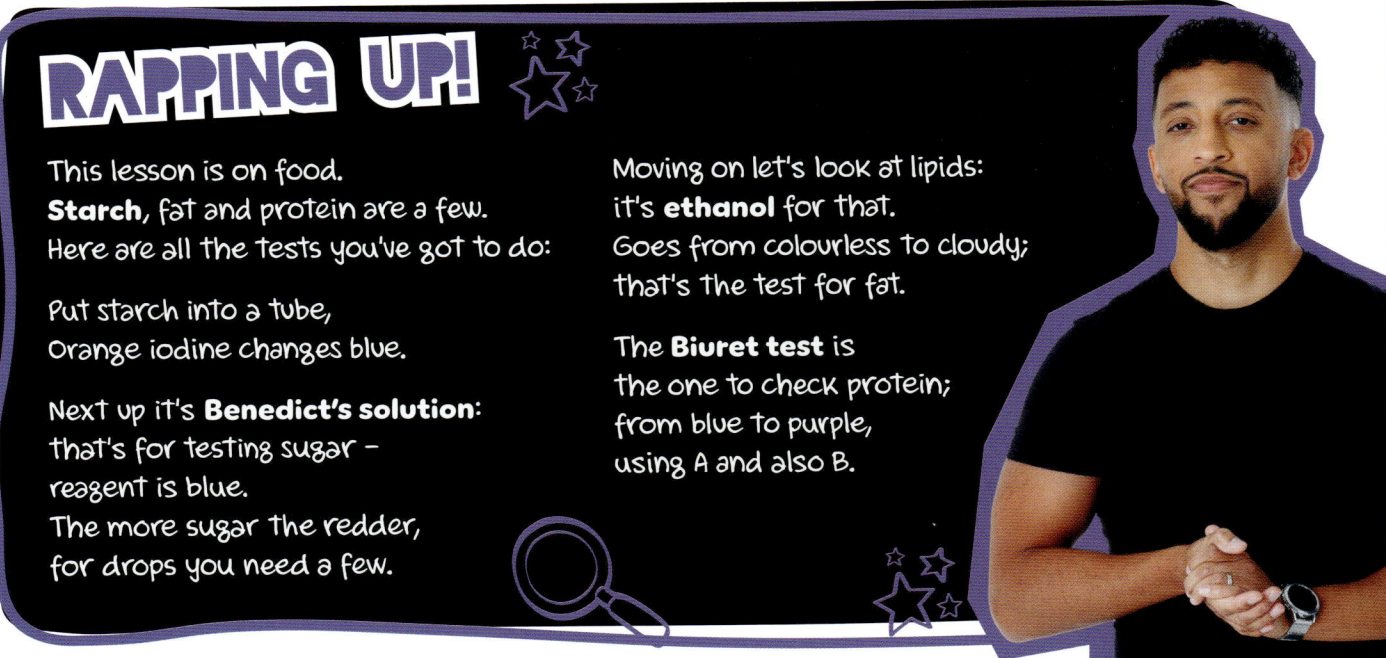

RAPPING UP!

This lesson is on food.
Starch, fat and protein are a few.
Here are all the tests you've got to do:

Put starch into a tube,
Orange iodine changes blue.

Next up it's **Benedict's solution**:
that's for testing sugar –
reagent is blue.
The more sugar the redder,
for drops you need a few.

Moving on let's look at lipids:
it's **ethanol** for that.
Goes from colourless to cloudy;
that's the test for fat.

The **Biuret test** is
the one to check protein;
from blue to purple,
using A and also B.

Digestion

Key terms

- Bile
- Carbohydrases
- Digestion
- Digestive enzymes
- Lipases
- Proteases

Digestive enzymes

Digestion is the process by which large insoluble food molecules are broken down.

Digestive enzymes play a key role in this process. They convert food into small soluble molecules that can be absorbed into the bloodstream.

- **Carbohydrases** break down carbohydrates into simple sugars.
- **Proteases** break down proteins into amino acids.
- **Lipases** break down lipids (fats) into glycerol and fatty acids.

The products of digestion are used to synthesise (build) new carbohydrates, lipids and proteins, which are used for growth and repair. Some glucose is used in respiration.

Carbohydrases

Carbohydrases break down carbohydrates into simple sugars, which are used for energy. This happens in the mouth and the small intestine.

Amylase is a carbohydrase that breaks down starch into glucose. Amylase is produced by the salivary glands, the pancreas and the small intestine.

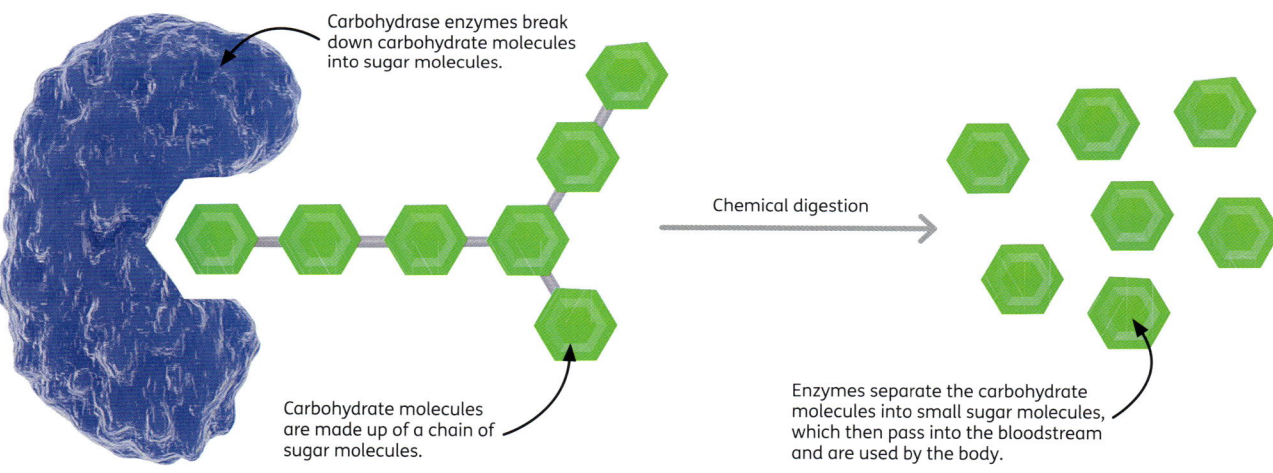

Proteases

Protein digestion occurs in the stomach and small intestine. Here, proteases break down proteins into amino acids, which are used for growth and repair. Proteases are produced by the stomach, the pancreas and the small intestine.

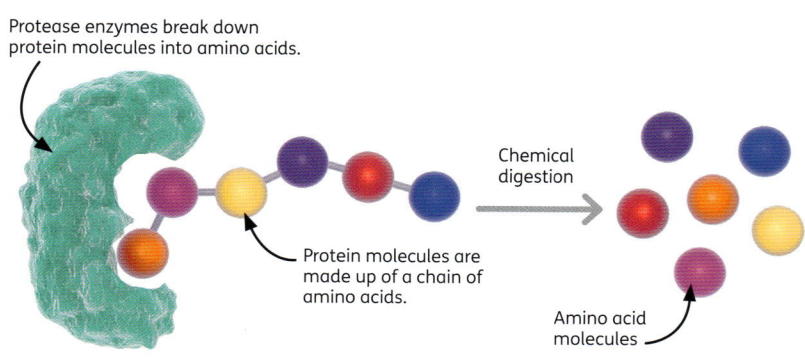

Organisation

Bile

Bile is made in the liver and stored in the gall bladder. It is released into the small intestine where it has two important functions:

- It is alkaline so it neutralises hydrochloric acid from the stomach.
- It emulsifies fat by breaking the fat into small droplets, increasing the surface area.

The alkaline conditions and large surface area increase the rate at which lipases can break down fat.

Breaking down fats

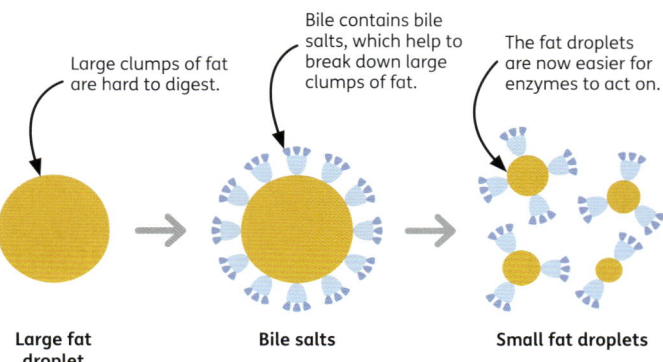

Lipases

Lipases break down lipids into fatty acids and glycerol, in the small intestine. Once absorbed, these can be turned back into lipids and used for insulation or as a store of energy. Lipases are produced by the pancreas and the small intestine.

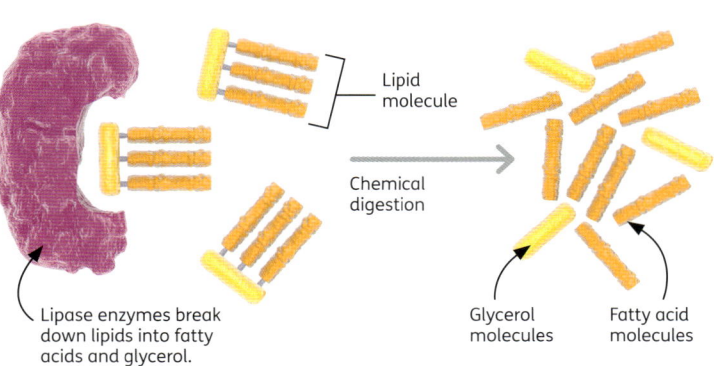

RAPPING UP!

Everything stops when I start my lesson,
I break things down; I'm like **digestion**.
This takes place inside this section –
from the mouth down to the large intestine.

Teeth chew food, it's quite impressing,
amylase enzymes start digesting
starch into maltose, it's finessing,
now into a bolus it's compressing.

Oesophagus here, it's hollow,
take a couple chews, then the food's swallowed.
Down into the **stomach** now it follows;
hydrochloric acid disinfects all real thorough.

Small intestine comes next,
its job is to absorb with no stress
food molecules through the villi no less,
duodenum first and ileum next.

Liver makes bile – to break fats –
emulsification we call that.
The gall bladder holds all the bile back;
drops it in the duodenum
when it sees the level lack.

The pancreas makes these **enzymes**,
water absorbed in the large intestine.
The last part now is really quite painless;
builds in here then drops out your anus!

Organisation

Enzyme Action

Key terms

- Active site
- Catalyst
- Denatured
- Enzyme
- Substrate

Science skills

To calculate the rate of an enzyme-controlled reaction when investigating pH:

Rate of reaction = $\dfrac{1}{\text{Time}}$

Enzymes

Enzymes are biological **catalysts** – large protein molecules that speed up chemical reactions without being used up themselves. This means they can be used over and over again.

Some enzymes, like digestive enzymes, break down large substrate molecules into smaller ones.

Others join small molecules together to form larger ones, such as in the synthesis of carbohydrates, proteins and lipids.

The molecules that enzymes change are called **substrates**. These fit into a specific part of the enzyme – the **active site** – due to their complementary shape.

Enzymes and temperature

Different enzymes work best at different temperatures. The temperature at which an enzyme catalyses a reaction the fastest is its optimum temperature.

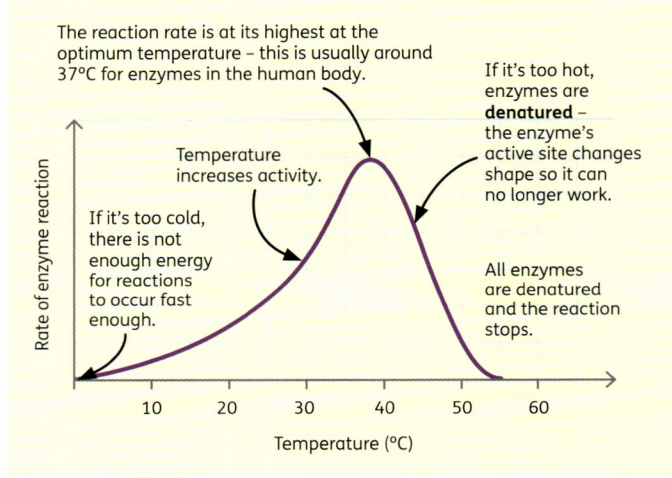

The reaction rate is at its highest at the optimum temperature – this is usually around 37°C for enzymes in the human body.

Temperature increases activity.

If it's too cold, there is not enough energy for reactions to occur fast enough.

If it's too hot, enzymes are **denatured** – the enzyme's active site changes shape so it can no longer work.

All enzymes are denatured and the reaction stops.

Lock and key model

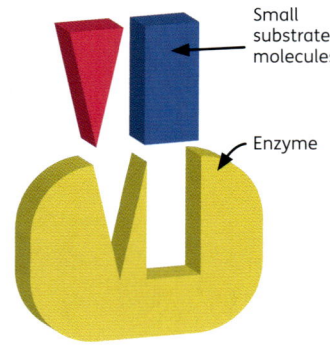

The lock and key model explains how enzymes work. Each enzyme has a uniquely shaped active site (the lock), which only a specifically shaped substrate (the key) can fit into. This means each type of enzyme can only catalyse one reaction.

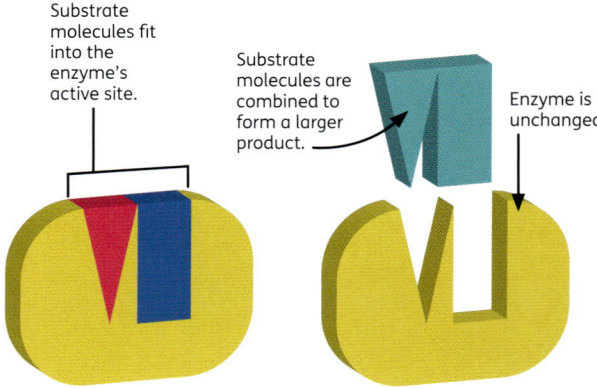

Small substrate molecules

Enzyme

Substrate molecules fit into the enzyme's active site.

Substrate molecules are combined to form a larger product.

Enzyme is unchanged

1. The molecule that an enzyme acts on is called the substrate. Enzyme and substrate molecules have shapes that complement each other.

2. The enzyme's unique shape enables it to form a temporary bond with the substrates. The two substrates molecules then react with each other.

3. The new, larger product separates from the enzyme. The enzyme is unchanged at the end of the reaction and is used over and over again.

Organisation

Science skills

The effect of pH on enzyme activity can be investigated by measuring the time it takes amylase to break down starch into glucose, under different pH conditions:

1. Place some drops of iodine into the wells of a spotting tile.
2. Place starch solution, amylase solution and pH buffer solution (which keeps the pH stable) into a water bath set at 37°C.
3. Leave until the solutions reach 3°C, the optimum temperature.
4. Mix the three solutions and start the timer.
5. Every 30 seconds, use a pipette to remove some of the reaction solution and add it to the next well in the spotting tile. Continue until the iodine no longer turns blue-black (see page 22).

Repeat steps 1–5 with different pH buffers. The sample that takes the shortest amount of time to stop testing positive for starch indicates the amylase's optimum pH.

RAPPING UP!

Let's take a look at enzymes, oh my.
They speed up rates of reaction inside – enzymes.
Biological **catalysts**.
They ain't breaking or getting used up.

They can break down and break down every substrate
in the active site.
They make the rate go so high.

Only at the right temperature,
37 is perfect, 0 is slow and at over 45 they **denature**.

It's time that we talk about **pH**.
Lower than 6 then it slows down.
Higher than 8 is the same now.
Number 7 is optimal,
7 is just right.

Enzymes and pH

Different enzymes work best at different pH levels, for example:
- Pepsin (a digestive enzyme in the stomach) optimum = pH 2.
- Trypsin (a digestive enzyme in the small intestine) optimum = pH 8.

Extremely high or low pH values cause an enzyme to denature.

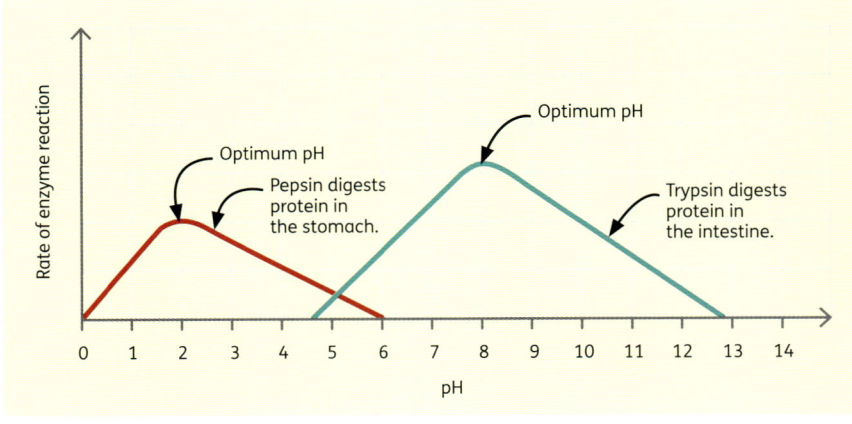

Organisation

Circulatory System

Key terms

- Artery
- Capillary
- Circulatory system
- Lumen
- Valve
- Vein

Key facts

- The **circulatory system** delivers nutrients and oxygen to every cell in the body. It also transports waste products to organs, which can remove them from the body.
- The circulatory system is made up of the heart, the blood and the blood vessels.
- There are three types of blood vessel: **arteries**, **veins** and **capillaries**.

Types of blood vessel

Blood vessels vary in size and structure depending on their function.

Blood vessel type	Artery	Vein	Capillary
Function	Carries blood away from the heart.	Carries blood back to the heart.	Links arteries to veins.
Structure	• Thick muscular walls to withstand high blood pressure. • An elastic layer to stretch as the blood surges through the narrow **lumen**.	• Thin layer of muscle and elastic as blood is carried under low pressure. • Large lumen to allow blood to flow easily. • Has valves to ensure that blood flows in one direction.	• Has very thin permeable walls so that substances can pass easily between blood and cells. • Very narrow so blood travels slowly, ensuring all oxygen diffuses into the body.
Cross-section	Small lumen	Large lumen	Very small lumen

Organisation

Double circulatory system

Humans and other mammals have a double circulatory system. This means that blood passes through the heart twice during one complete circuit of the body.

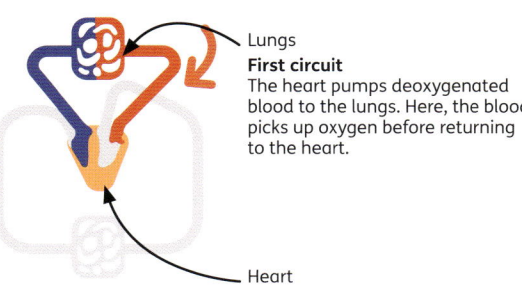

Lungs
First circuit
The heart pumps deoxygenated blood to the lungs. Here, the blood picks up oxygen before returning to the heart.

Heart

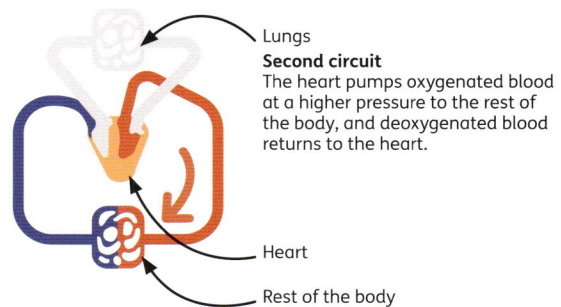

Lungs
Second circuit
The heart pumps oxygenated blood at a higher pressure to the rest of the body, and deoxygenated blood returns to the heart.

Heart

Rest of the body

Valves

Valves are flap-like structures.
- They open when blood pushes against them.
- They close when the blood flows back.

Pressure from body muscles around the veins also helps to keep the blood moving forwards.

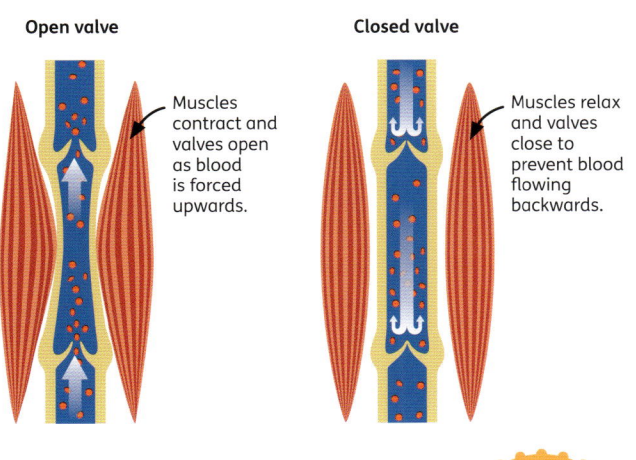

Open valve — Muscles contract and valves open as blood is forced upwards.

Closed valve — Muscles relax and valves close to prevent blood flowing backwards.

Science skills

Blood flows at different rates depending on the blood vessel it is travelling through.

To calculate blood flow:

$$\text{Rate of blood flow} = \frac{\text{Volume of blood}}{\text{Number of minutes}}$$

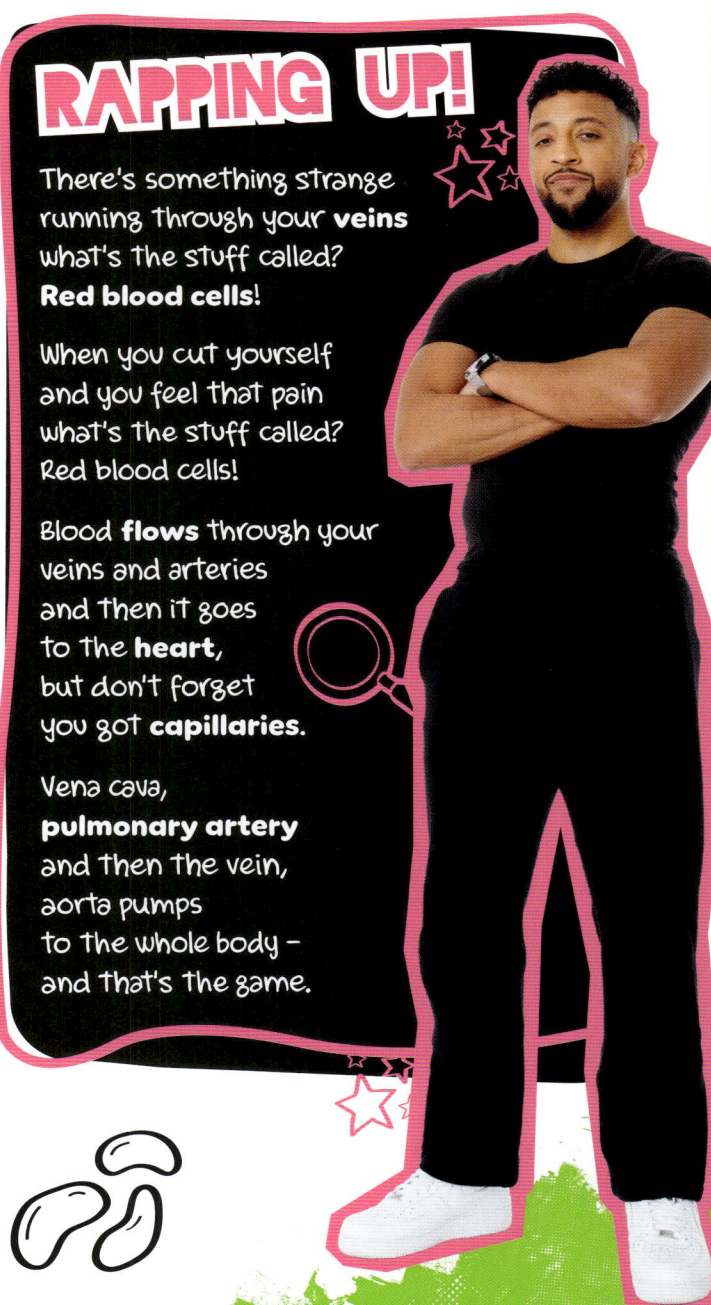

RAPPING UP!

There's something strange running through your **veins**
what's the stuff called?
Red blood cells!

When you cut yourself
and you feel that pain
what's the stuff called?
Red blood cells!

Blood **flows** through your
veins and arteries
and then it goes
to the **heart**,
but don't forget
you got **capillaries**.

Vena cava,
pulmonary artery
and then the vein,
aorta pumps
to the whole body –
and that's the game.

Organisation

Heart Structure

Key terms

- Aorta
- Atrium (plural atria)
- Pacemaker
- Pulmonary artery
- Pulmonary vein
- Vena cava
- Ventricle

Pacemaker

A group of specialised muscle cells in the right atrium act as a **pacemaker** – they control the heart's natural resting rate. An artificial pacemaker (a small electrical device) can be implanted in the chest and used to correct an irregular heart rate.

Structure of the heart

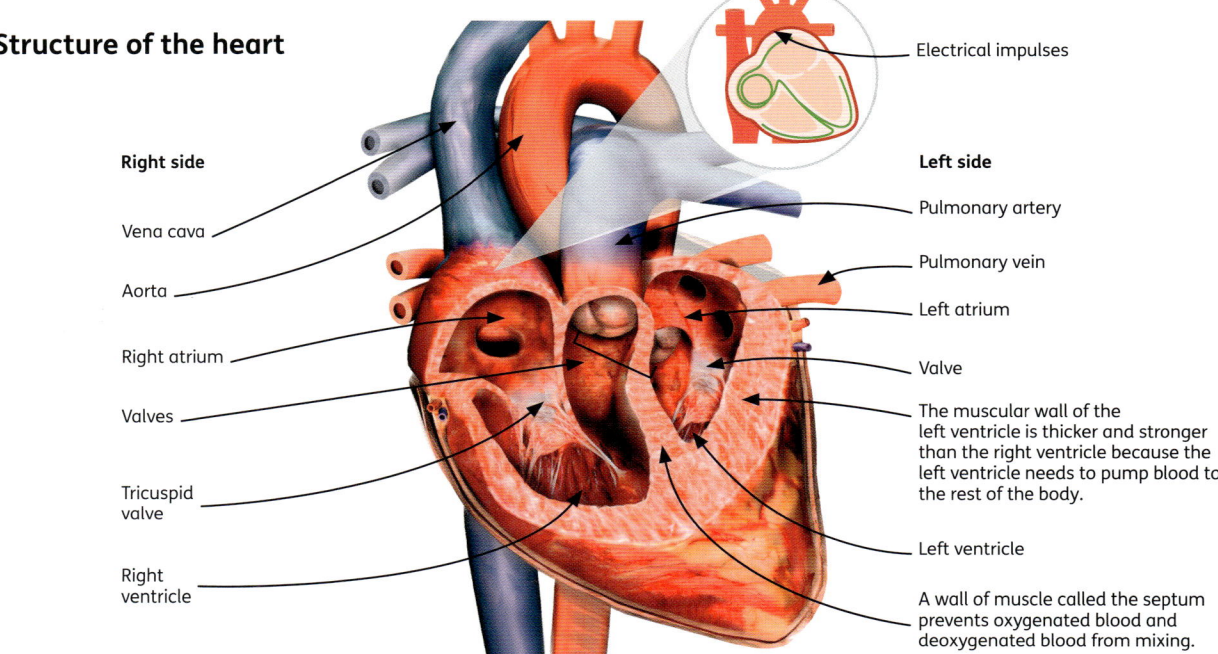

Structures in the heart

- The heart has four chambers:
  - Two small upper chambers called atria.
  - Two large lower chambers called ventricles.
- The atria receive blood from the lungs and body through two major veins:
  - The right atrium receives deoxygenated blood from the body through the vena cava.
  - The left atrium receives oxygenated blood from the lungs through the pulmonary vein.
- The atria contract to force blood into the ventricles.
- The ventricles contract to pump blood out of the heart and into the arteries:
  - The right ventricle pumps deoxygenated blood to the lungs through the pulmonary artery.
  - The left ventricle pumps oxygenated blood around the body through the aorta.
- Valves inside the heart ensure that blood flows in one direction.

Organisation

Science skills

Cardiac output is the total volume of blood that is pumped out of the heart every minute by the left ventricle.

The heart rate is the number of times the heart beats per minute (bpm). This can be measured by counting your pulse rate.

To calculate cardiac output:

Cardiac output = Stroke volume × Heart rate

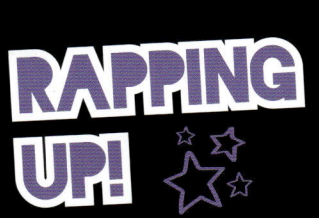

RAPPING UP!

4 Chambers, let's look at them all.
2 **Atriums** and 2 **ventricals**.
Left side is big and right side is small.
Count with me - 4 blood vessels.

Let me explain to you how this works.
Blood without O₂ enters first.
Into the right through the vena cava.
then it goes here - you see the **atria**?

Now to the ventrical. Sharply
needs to get out the **pulmonary artery**.
From there it goes to the lungs.
It's got O₂ so blood takes some.

Now back to the heart again.
This time through the **pulmonary vein**.
Now the left side pumps way stronger
and sends it to the body out the aorta.

Blocked arteries

Coronary heart disease (CHD) occurs when fatty materials (such as cholesterol) build up in the coronary arteries. This narrows them and reduces blood flow, reducing the heart's oxygen supply.

If the artery is completely blocked, it can cause a heart attack.

If this happens to the arteries in the brain, it can starve the brain of oxygen, causing a stroke.

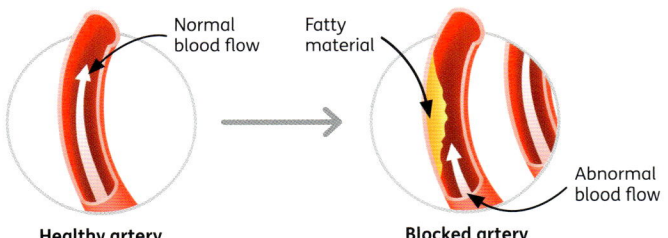

Treating coronary heart disease

Treatment	Stent	Statin	Mechanical or biological valves	Heart transplant
Benefits	Metal mesh keeps the blocked artery open.	Reduces blood cholesterol – slows the build-up of fatty material in the arteries.	Replaces faulty heart valves that do not open properly or leak.	New fully functioning organ.
Risks	• Surgery • Infection	• Liver and kidney problems	• Surgery • Infection • Rejection (biological) • Risk of clots (mechanical)	• Surgery • Infection • Rejection • Long wait for donor

Artificial hearts are occasionally used to keep patients alive while waiting for a heart transplant, or to allow the heart to rest as an aid to recovery.

Diseases, Risk Factors and Cancer

Key terms

- Cancer
- Communicable disease
- Disease
- Health
- Non-communicable disease
- Risk factor

Key facts

- Health is the state of a person's physical, mental and social wellbeing.
- A disease is any condition that stops part of the body working properly or makes a person feel unwell.
- Diseases caused by infectious microorganisms (pathogens) are called communicable diseases, for example measles and HIV (see page 42).
- Diseases that are not caused by infectious microorganisms are called non-communicable. They cannot be spread, for example heart disease and diabetes.
- Diseases are major causes of ill health, but factors like diet, stress and exercise can also have a large effect.

Interaction of diseases

Different types of disease may interact. For example:

- Immune system faults mean a person is more likely to suffer from infectious diseases.
- Viruses living in cells can initiate some cancers.
- Immune reactions initially caused by a pathogen can trigger allergies like skin rashes and asthma.
- Physical ill health can lead to depression.

Lifestyle diseases

Improvements in healthcare have reduced the incidence of communicable diseases in many parts of the world. However, the number of people dying from non-communicable diseases has risen. Many of these diseases are affected by a person's lifestyle.

Deaths by non-transmissible diseases in people under the age of 70

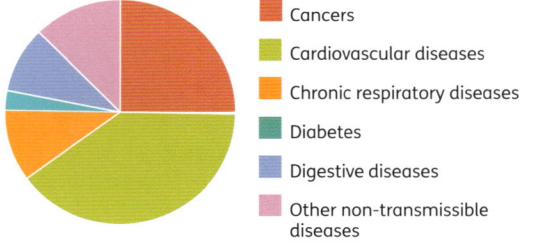

- Cancers
- Cardiovascular diseases
- Chronic respiratory diseases
- Diabetes
- Digestive diseases
- Other non-transmissible diseases

Risk factors

Risk factors are linked to an increased rate of a disease.

They can be lifestyle choices present in the environment or due to a person's age, sex or genetic makeup.

Some risk factors have been proved to cause disease. These are some examples:

- Poor diet, smoking and lack of exercise increase the risk of cardiovascular disease.
- Obesity increases the likelihood of type 2 diabetes.
- Alcohol damages the liver (cirrhosis) and brain function.
- Smoking increases the risk of lung disease and lung cancer.
- Smoking and alcohol harm unborn babies.

Organisation

Science skills

The waist to hip ratio indicates how much fat a person has around their abdomen. A ratio of more than 0.9 increases the risk of heart disease, type 2 diabetes, and other conditions linked to being overweight.

To calculate waist to hip ratio:

$$\text{Waist to hip ratio} = \frac{\text{Waist circumference}}{\text{Hip circumference}}$$

Cancer

Normal body cells grow and divide at a controlled rate. But if something goes wrong, cells may divide uncontrollably causing tumours.

- **Benign tumours:** growths of abnormal cells that are contained in one area, usually within a membrane. They do not invade other parts of the body.
- **Malignant tumours (cancer):** invade neighbouring tissues and spread to different parts of the body in the blood where they may form secondary tumours.

Causes of cancer

Cancer risk factors include genes, diet and exposure to chemicals called carcinogens, such as those in cigarette smoke.

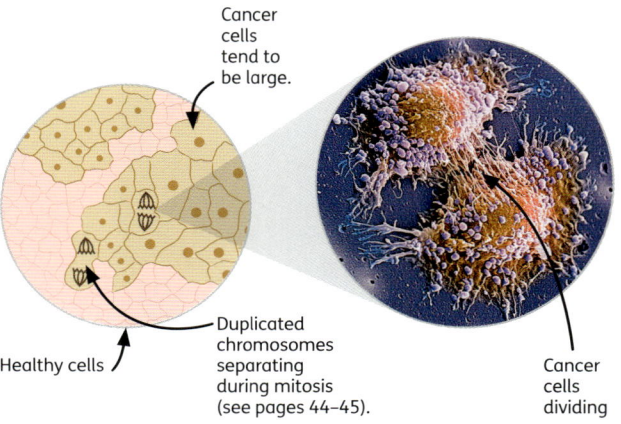

Cancer cells tend to be large.
Healthy cells
Duplicated chromosomes separating during mitosis (see pages 44–45).
Cancer cells dividing

RAPPING UP!

We all want to smoke, drink and eat MacD's without getting **cancer and heart disease**.
Now listen to my raps and please believe
I'm here to teach facts, I ain't here to preach.

I'm a list the five types of diseases (cancer, diabetes, genetic, heart disease, neurological).

Doing these things and your risk increases (poor diet, low exercise, smoking, alcohol, drugs, stress).
I'll take you through the topic now so completely
but I teach so sweet you'll get **diabetes**.

Smoking clogs up your arteries;
tar, carbon monoxide and nicotine.
Strokes ain't a joke, but you see the fat,
so it's either that or a **heart attack**.

How do we evaluate these risk factors
When do we find out what causes cancer?
It's all to do with cause and effect:
when more folk smoke then more are dead.

If you didn't know, it's time you're told,
it's when cells grow with no control.
With this disease, there are two types:
one's **malignant** and one's **benign**.

Malignant spreads and it grows real quick.
With **metastasis**, it makes you sick.
Benign grows slow and it's self-contained.
Docs can remove it from the membrane.

The liver breaks down your alcohol.
Drinking too much will take its toll.
This ain't news, now I think you know this,
hepatitis and/or cirrhosis.

I've talked about these but not Mac D's.
Too much fat will make us obese.
Take care now that's it from me.
Do your best to live to 93.

Organisation

Plant Tissues, Organs and Systems

Key terms

- Epidermis
- Palisade mesophyll
- Phloem vessels
- Spongy mesophyll
- Stoma (plural stomata)
- Translocation
- Transpiration
- Xylem vessels

Plant organisation

- The main organs of a plant are the root, stem, leaf, flower and fruit.
- The roots, stem and leaves form an organ system, which transports substances around the plant.

Leaves are made up of several plant tissues:

- Epidermis: a transparent layer of cells around the leaf.
- Palisade mesophyll: where photosynthesis takes place.
- Spongy mesophyll: where gas exchange takes place.
- Xylem vessels: transport water and minerals.
- Phloem vessels: transport dissolved sugars.
- Stomata are small holes in the leaf, which let in carbon dioxide and let out oxygen and water vapour.

Structure of a leaf

A leaf is adapted for photosynthesis by having a large surface area and lots of chloroplasts near its upper surface. Although it may look thin, a leaf is made up of several layers of cells.

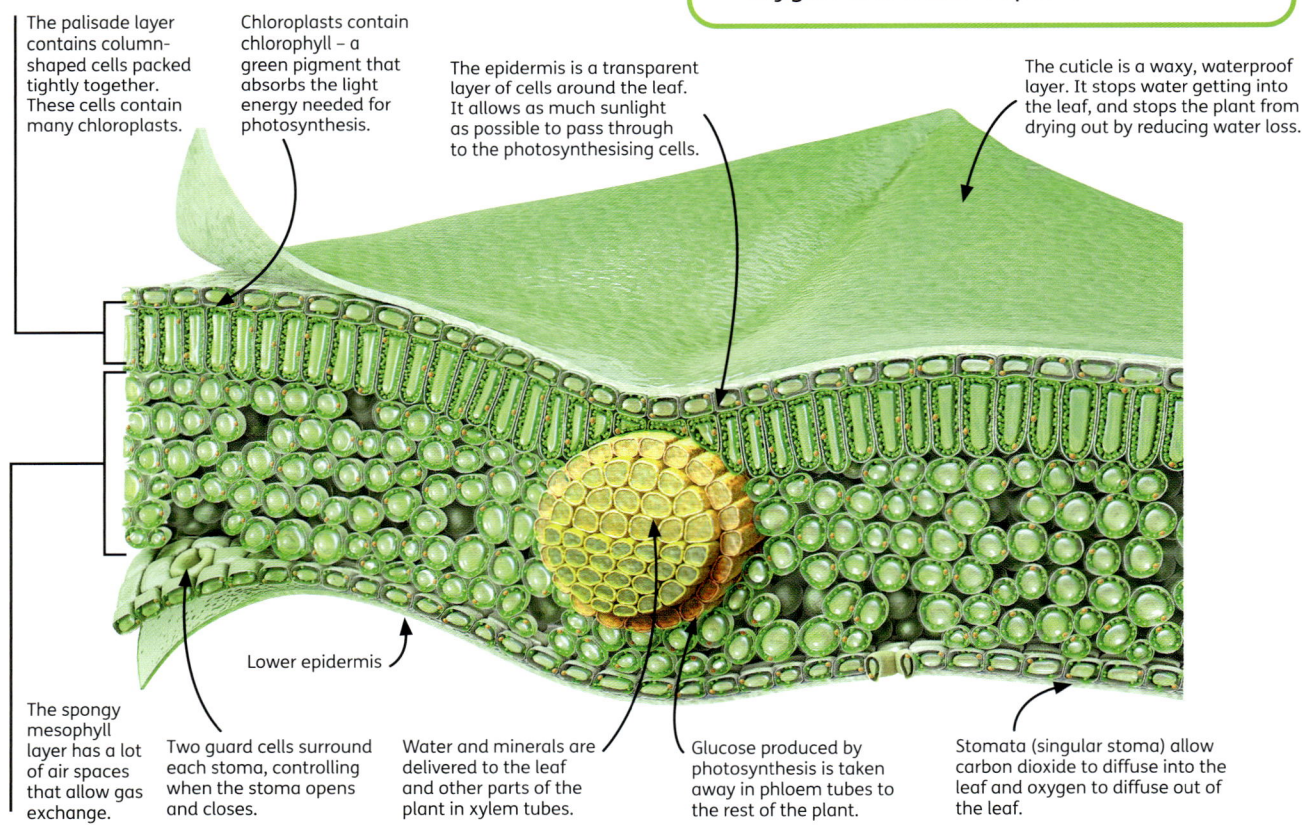

The palisade layer contains column-shaped cells packed tightly together. These cells contain many chloroplasts.

Chloroplasts contain chlorophyll – a green pigment that absorbs the light energy needed for photosynthesis.

The epidermis is a transparent layer of cells around the leaf. It allows as much sunlight as possible to pass through to the photosynthesising cells.

The cuticle is a waxy, waterproof layer. It stops water getting into the leaf, and stops the plant from drying out by reducing water loss.

The spongy mesophyll layer has a lot of air spaces that allow gas exchange.

Two guard cells surround each stoma, controlling when the stoma opens and closes.

Lower epidermis

Water and minerals are delivered to the leaf and other parts of the plant in xylem tubes.

Glucose produced by photosynthesis is taken away in phloem tubes to the rest of the plant.

Stomata (singular stoma) allow carbon dioxide to diffuse into the leaf and oxygen to diffuse out of the leaf.

Organisation 35

Key facts

- Guard cells open and close stomata to control gas exchange and water loss.
- Xylem tubes and phloem tubes form continuous tubes for liquids to flow through the plant.
- The upward movement of water to all parts of the plant is called **transpiration**.
- The movement of sugars around the plant through the phloem is called **translocation**.

Opening and closing of stomata

Stomata are mainly found on the underside of a leaf, shaded from sunlight, so less water is lost through transpiration (see page 36).

When conditions for photosynthesis are poor, such as when it is dark, water passes out of the guard cells. This makes them **flaccid** and causes the stoma to close.

When plenty of light and water are available, water passes into the guard cells by osmosis (see pages 52–53). This makes the guard cells **turgid**. As they swell, they bend, causing the stoma to open.

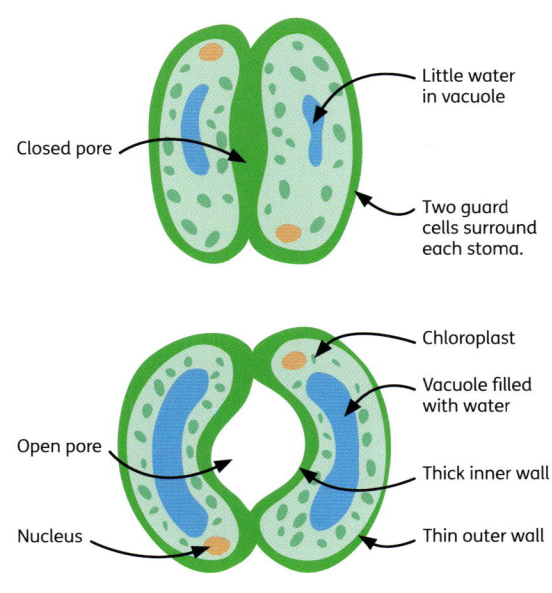

Transport tissues

Xylem

Xylem tubes transport water and mineral ions from the roots to the stems and leaves.

The water travels in one direction – upwards. Xylem tubes are made from dead cells that have joined together. There is no cytoplasm. The hollow tubes created are strengthened by lignin.

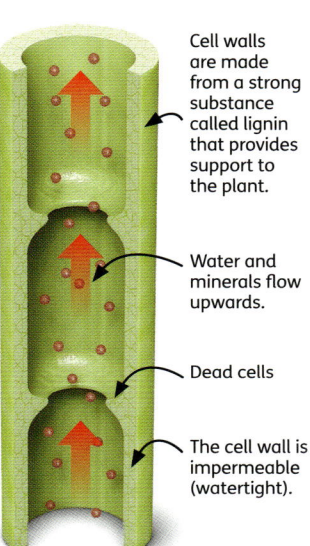

Phloem

Phloem tissue transports dissolved sugars from the leaves to the rest of the plant for immediate use or storage. This is called translocation. Substances move in both directions. Phloem tubes are made of living elongated (stretched) cells. Small pores (holes) in the end walls form sieve plates, which allow the dissolved sugars produced during photosynthesis to pass between the cells.

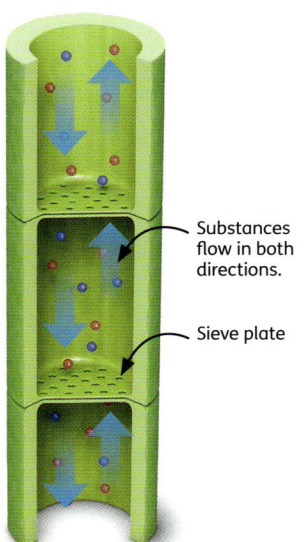

Factors Affecting Transpiration

Key terms

- Transpiration
- Transpiration stream

Key facts

- Plants lose water through the stomata in their leaves by evaporation.
- The loss of water from the leaves draws more water up through the plant, through the xylem. This process is called **transpiration**.
- Four factors affect the rate of transpiration: temperature, humidity, wind speed and light intensity.

Transpiration stream

When a plant loses water through its leaves, the water is replaced through the roots. The uninterrupted stream of water from the roots to the leaves is called the **transpiration stream**.

Water evaporates into the air.

Open stoma

1. Stomata are tiny holes in leaves through which water evaporates. Carbon dioxide enters the leaves through these holes, and oxygen diffuses out.

Evaporation of water from the leaf pulls more water up the xylem.

Mesophyll cells have damp cell walls.

2. Leaves contain spongy mesophyll cells that are covered with a film of moisture. When this moisture evaporates, it diffuses out through the stomata.

Water rises through the stem.

Xylem

3. Tiny tubes called xylem tubes run through the stem. The loss of water from the leaves pulls more water through these tubes, replacing what has been lost from the mesophyll cells.

Water enters the roots by osmosis.

4. The roots are covered in specialised cells that stick out into the soil. They have a large surface area to absorb both water and minerals from the soil.

Organisation

Science skills

A potometer estimates transpiration rates by measuring how quickly a plant takes up water.

As water is taken up by the plant, an air bubble moves along a capillary tube.

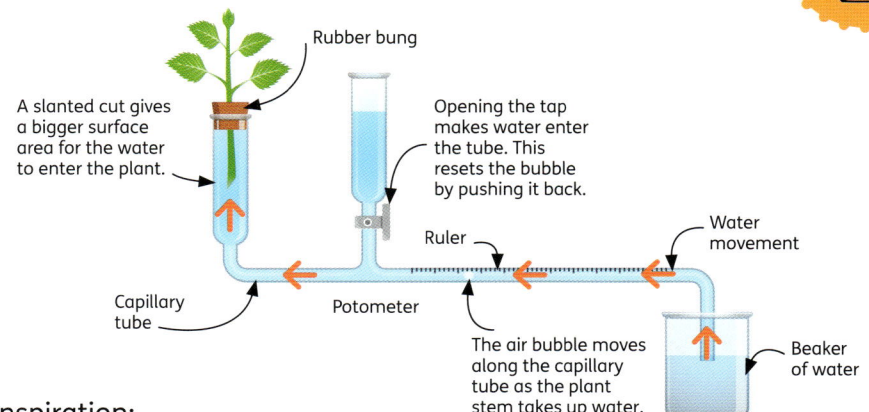

To calculate the rate of transpiration:

$$\text{Rate of transpiration (mm/s)} = \frac{\text{Distance moved by bubble (in millimetres)}}{\text{Time taken (in seconds)}}$$

Factors affecting transpiration

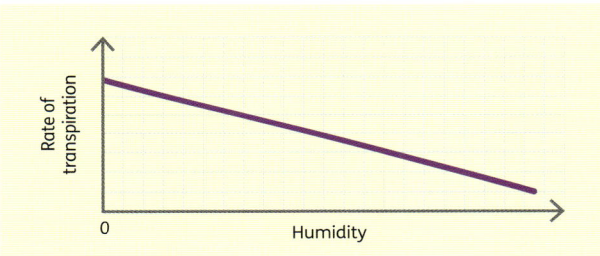

Humidity
Increasing humidity (the amount of water vapour in the air) decreases the rate of transpiration, and the concentration gradient of water between the leaf and the air becomes less steep.

Wind speed
Increasing wind speed increases the rate of transpiration, as the water vapour that has diffused out of the leaves is moved away quickly. This maintains a steep water concentration gradient between the water in the leaf and its environment.

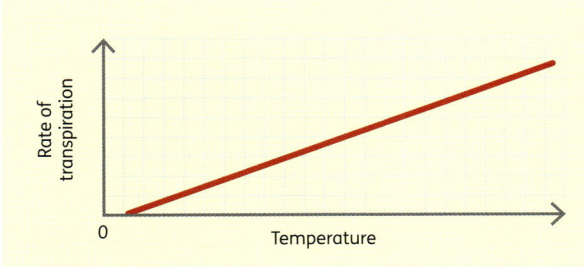

Temperature
Increasing temperature increases the rate of transpiration, as water evaporates faster in higher temperatures.

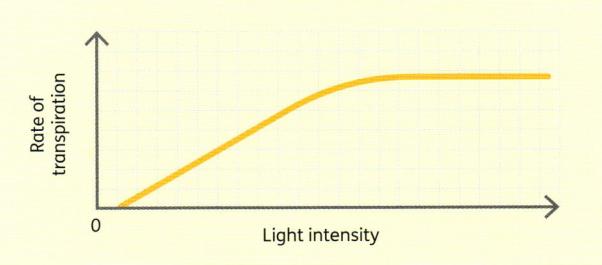

Light intensity
As light intensity increases, the rate of photosynthesis increases. This causes stomata to open so enough carbon dioxide can diffuse into the leaf. However, water also diffuses out.

Brain Booster

Organisation Recap Quiz

 Find a pen and paper and work through these revision questions.

1. Which of the following are organs? Select all that apply.
   brain   muscle cell   circulatory system   kidney   sperm

2. Explain why blood is a tissue.

3. Which of the following reagents is used to test food for protein?
   iodine   Benedict's solution   Biuret's solution

4. Describe the role of the following types of enzyme in digestion:
   a) carbohydrases   b) proteases   c) lipases

5. State one role of bile.

6. Explain why enzymes can only break down one type of substrate.

7. Describe the structure of:
   a) an artery   b) a vein   c) a capillary

8. Name **four** treatments for coronary heart disease.

9. Explain what is meant by cancer.

10. State the tissue in a leaf where photosynthesis takes place.

11. Describe translocation.

12. Name **four** factors that affect the rate of transpiration.

Check your answers on page **109**.

Infection and Response

At the end of this chapter, you should be able to:

- ✓ Describe the different types of pathogen and explain how they cause disease.
- ✓ Explain how communicable diseases are spread.
- ✓ Describe how the spread of infectious diseases can be reduced or prevented.
- ✓ Describe the symptoms of some diseases.
- ✓ Describe the physical human defence systems against pathogens.
- ✓ Explain how the immune system helps protect the body.
- ✓ Explain how vaccinations work to prevent illness.
- ✓ Describe the use of antibiotics and painkillers in treating disease.
- ✓ Explain the stages in the development of new drugs.
- ✓ Describe some plant diseases and plant defences.

Infection and Response

Pathogens

Key terms

- Bacterium
- Communicable (infectious) diseases
- Fungus
- Non-communicable disease
- Pathogen
- Protist
- Vector

Types of disease

Diseases stop our bodies working well. Pathogens are microorganisms that cause **communicable diseases**, which can spread between organisms. **Non-communicable diseases** cannot be spread. There are four types of pathogens: **bacteria**, **fungi**, viruses and protists.

Bacterial diseases

Disease	Typical symptoms	Spread	Prevention
Salmonella food poisoning	Fever, abdominal cramps, vomiting, diarrhoea	Contaminated food or poor hygiene	Vaccination of poultry, thorough food cooking
Cholera	Diarrhoea	Contaminated water	Water purification
Tuberculosis (TB)	Lung damage	Airborne droplets	Ventilation, masks
Helicobacter	Ulcers in stomach lining	Food	Hand washing, using clean water in food preparation
Gonorrhoea	Thick yellow/green pus from vagina or penis, pain when peeing	Sexual contact	Use of condoms, antibiotic treatment
Chlamydia	Pain when passing urine	Sexual contact	Use of condoms

Salmonella bacteria

Salmonella bacteria can survive the acid in the stomach. They release toxins that cause the symptoms.

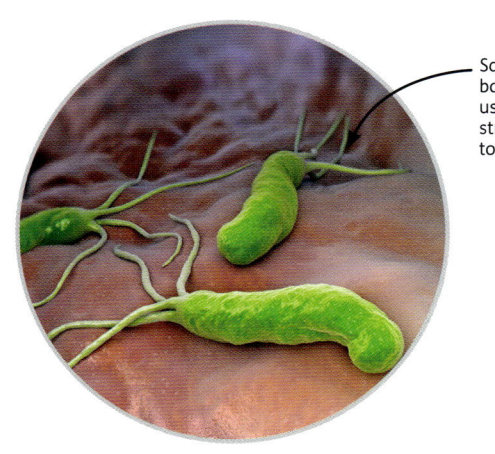

Salmonella bacteria use their hairlike strands (flagella) to move.

Infection and Response

Fungal and protist diseases

Disease	Pathogen	Typical symptoms	Spread	Prevention
Athlete's foot	Fungus	Itchy skin between toes	Spores on wet floors	Keep feet clean and dry
Malaria	Protist (called Plasmodium)	Repeating episodes of fever	Mosquitoes are the vectors	Mosquito nets, avoiding mosquito bites, draining stagnant water to stop mosquitoes breeding

Malaria transmission

1. A female mosquito infected with Plasmodium searches for a victim to bite.
2. The mosquito bites a person. The insect is the vector – it transfers the protist to a person.
3. The person's liver cells become infected.
4. The person's red blood cells become infected.
5. A different mosquito bites the infected person.
6. A different person is infected.

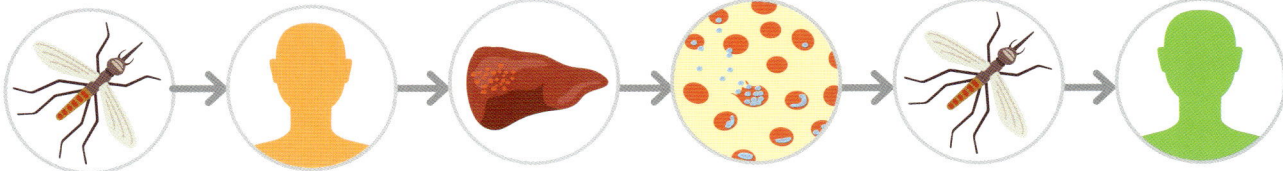

RAPPING UP!

Microbes are small, not all of them are calm.
If you catch a pathogen, then that will cause you harm.
Starting with **bacteria,** don't meant to cause alarm
but they divide so rapidly, you better wash your palms.

Salmonella's one – another's gonorrhea.
Moving swiftly on – it's time I show you more ideas.
Fungus is another type of microbe that you hear.
Rose black spot's a pathogen and **yeast** for making beer.

This next one you know - we call it a **virus.**
They can't live up on their own. A host cell is required.
If they were a person, you would know they were a liar.
HIV is one and tobacco mosaic virus.

Protist diseases are the easiest, it really is.
Remember malaria and now you are a genius.
How do they all spread, and why aren't we all dead?
I'm about to cover that so get this in your head.

Pathogens, they get about when folks hygiene is shocking.
Droplet - infection? That's from sneezing or coughing.
Contaminated food or drink – a reason there for washing.
If you catch a bad one, then you're leaving in a coffin.

Infection and Response

Viral Pathogens

Key terms

- AIDS
- Ebola
- HIV
- Lytic pathway
- Measles
- Virus
- Lysogenic pathway

A typical virus particle

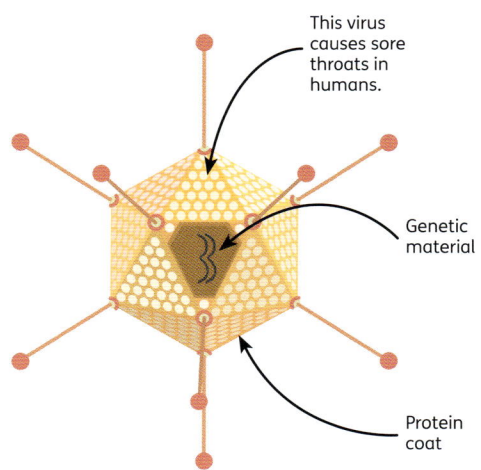

This virus causes sore throats in humans.
Genetic material
Protein coat

Virus particles are simple structures that invade host cells and replicate inside them, often destroying them. Examples of viral diseases are measles, HIV and Ebola.

Measles

- Symptoms: red skin rash, fever.
- Complications: can be fatal (for example brain infection).
- Transmission: airborne droplets from sneezes and coughs.
- Prevention: vaccination at a young age.

Measles symptoms

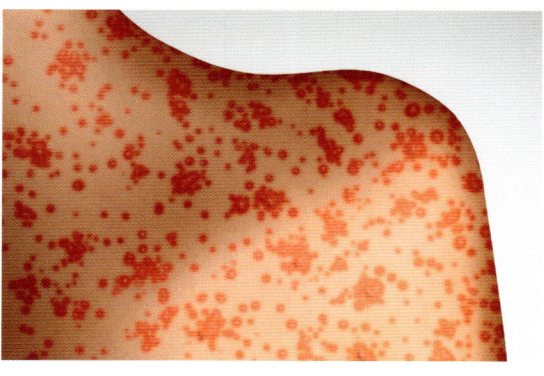

HIV

- Symptoms: flu-like illness shortly after infection.
- Complications: if untreated, it causes **AIDS**.
- Transmission: body fluids (for example sexual contact, drug users sharing needles).
- Prevention: using condoms. Needle exchange programmes.

HIV virus structure
The virus particle is covered in a membrane that helps to disguise it from the immune system.

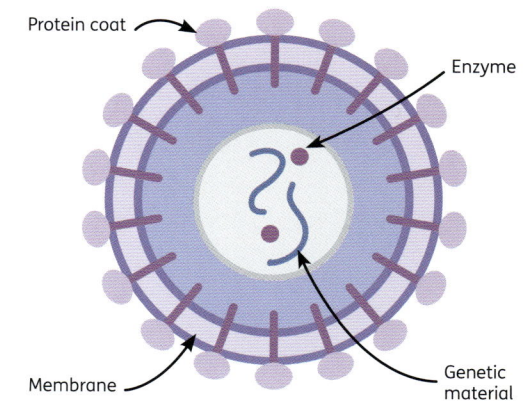

Protein coat
Enzyme
Membrane
Genetic material

Infection and Response

Ebola

- Symptoms: haemorrhagic fever (internal bleeding, fever, vomiting).
- Complications: often fatal.
- Transmission: body fluids.
- Prevention: isolation of infected people, protective clothing.

Ebola virus particles

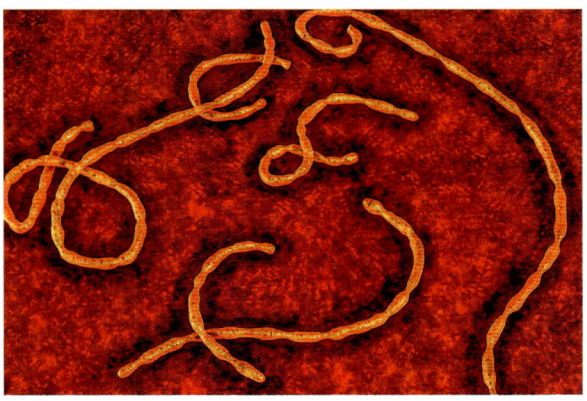

Virus lifecyles

Viruses can use two different pathways to replicate. The **lytic pathway** is the one that causes disease symptoms, when virus particles replicate inside a cell and then burst out of it. However, many viruses hide inside a host for long periods of time by using a **lysogenic pathway**, in which their genetic material becomes part of the host's DNA.

In summary, while the lytic cycle is characterised by the rapid replication and release of viruses leading to the destruction of the host cell, the lysogenic cycle involves the integration of the viral genome into the host DNA, allowing for a more prolonged interaction with the host without immediate destruction.

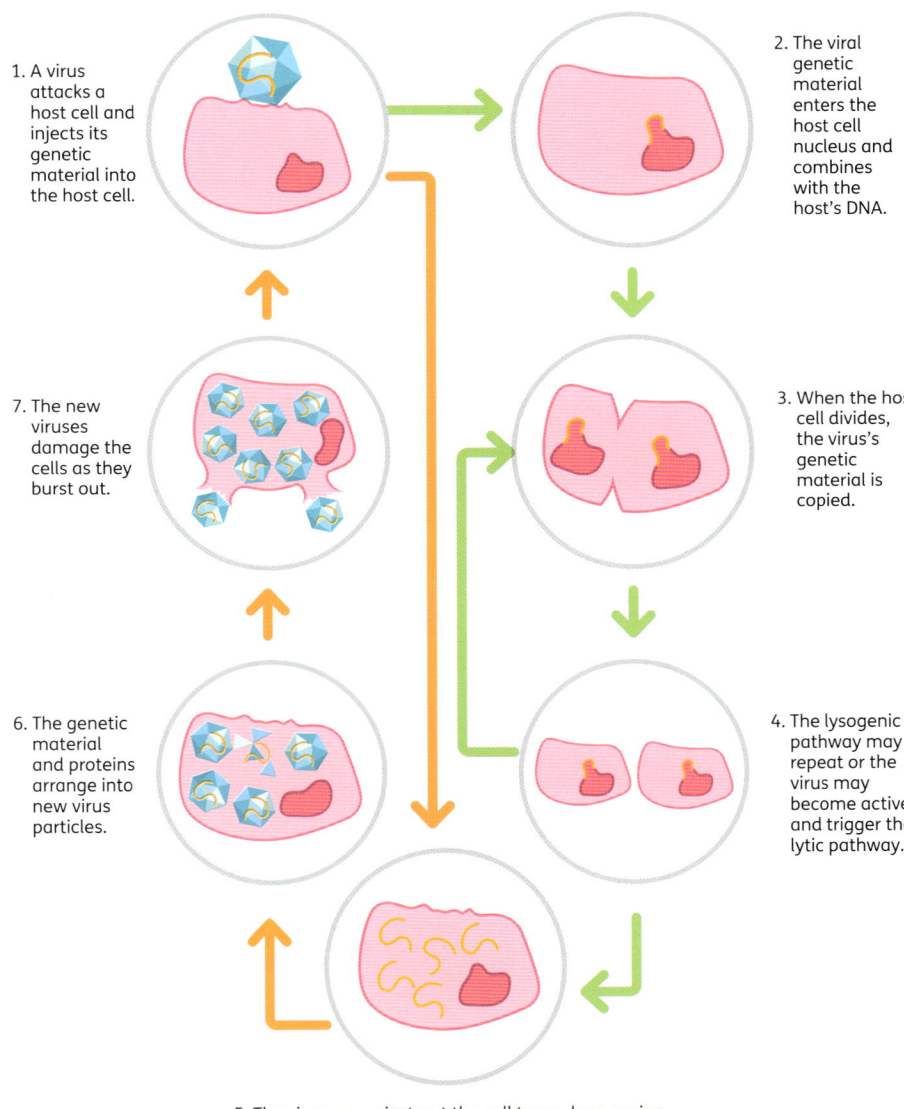

1. A virus attacks a host cell and injects its genetic material into the host cell.
2. The viral genetic material enters the host cell nucleus and combines with the host's DNA.
3. When the host cell divides, the virus's genetic material is copied.
4. The lysogenic pathway may repeat or the virus may become active and trigger the lytic pathway.
5. The virus genes instruct the cell to produce copies of the virus's genetic material and proteins.
6. The genetic material and proteins arrange into new virus particles.
7. The new viruses damage the cells as they burst out.

■ Lytic pathway   ■ Lysogenic pathway

Infection and Response

Human Defence Systems

Key terms

- Antibody
- Antitoxin
- Immunisation
- Lymphocyte
- Lysozyme
- Memory cell
- Phagocyte
- Vaccine

Non-specific defence systems

Defence	How it works
Skin	Overlapping cells on the skin surface stop pathogen entry. Scabs quickly seal any cuts.
Nose	Hairs and mucus trap pathogens.
Trachea and bronchi	Mucus traps pathogens. Cilia on cells sweep mucus to the oesophagus to be swallowed.
Stomach	Hydrochloric acid kills pathogens.
Lysozyme	An enzyme that can kill bacteria – found in tears, mucus and saliva.

Phagocytes and phagocytosis
White blood cells called phagocytes surround pathogens and digest them (in phagocytosis).

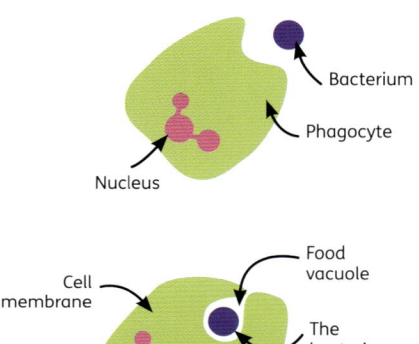

Lymphocytes

Antigens are shapes on a surface. They are normally proteins.

- White blood cells called **lymphocytes** have **antibodies** on their surfaces.
- If antigens on a pathogen fit into an antibody, that lymphocyte is activated and it multiplies.
- The new lymphocytes release free antibodies that attach to the pathogen.
- The antibodies inactivate the pathogen or mark it for destruction by **phagocytes**.
- **Antitoxins** are antibodies made in the same way to neutralise toxins made by bacteria.
- Some lymphocytes remain as **memory cells**, ready to release their antibodies quickly if the same pathogen enters again.

Lymphocyte action

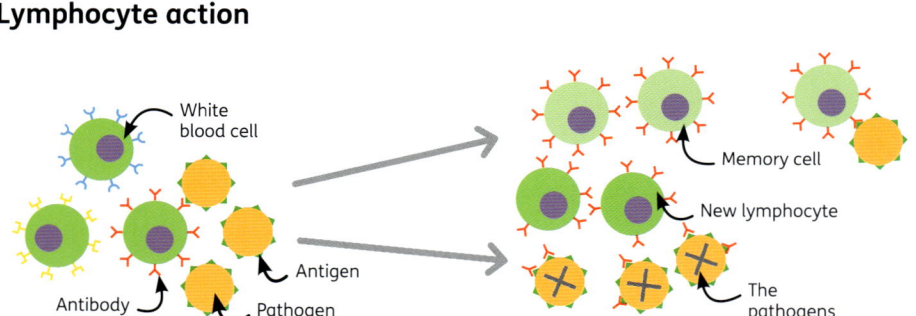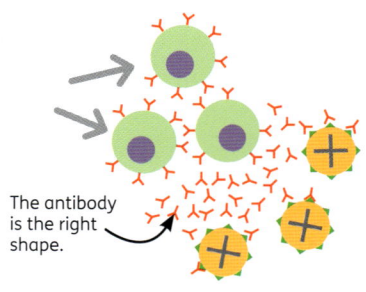

Pathogen activates a specific lymphocyte.

Free antibodies are released. Memory cells are created.

In the future, memory cells remain ready to release their antibodies quickly.

Infection and Response   45

Immune responses
Memory cells mean that the secondary response is quicker and produces more antibodies than the primary response. For this reason, people only get some diseases once.

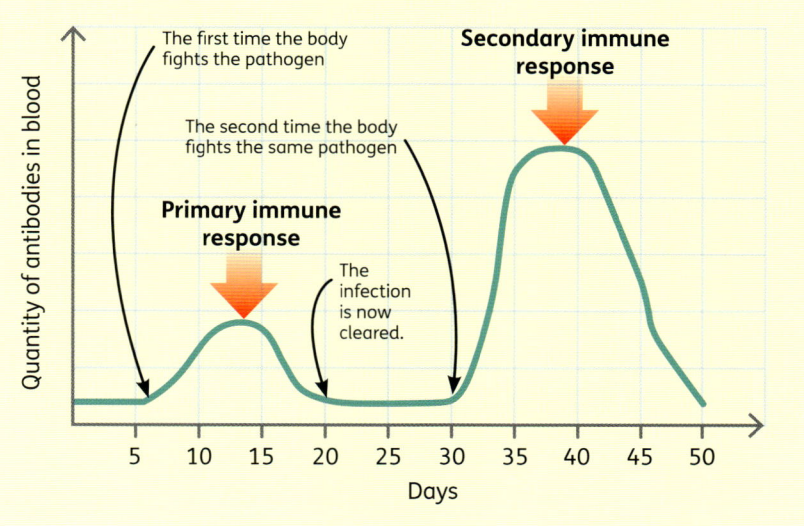

Key facts

- The body's defence systems keep pathogens out and destroy them if they get inside.
- Non-specific defence mechanisms aim to prevent any microorganism entering the body.
- White blood cells in the immune system destroy pathogens that get into the body.

Vaccination

In vaccination, a **vaccine** containing inactive pathogens or their antigens is put into the body to create memory cells. This causes immunity. If most people are **immunised**, the spread of that pathogen is reduced. This is called herd immunity.

Oral vaccination

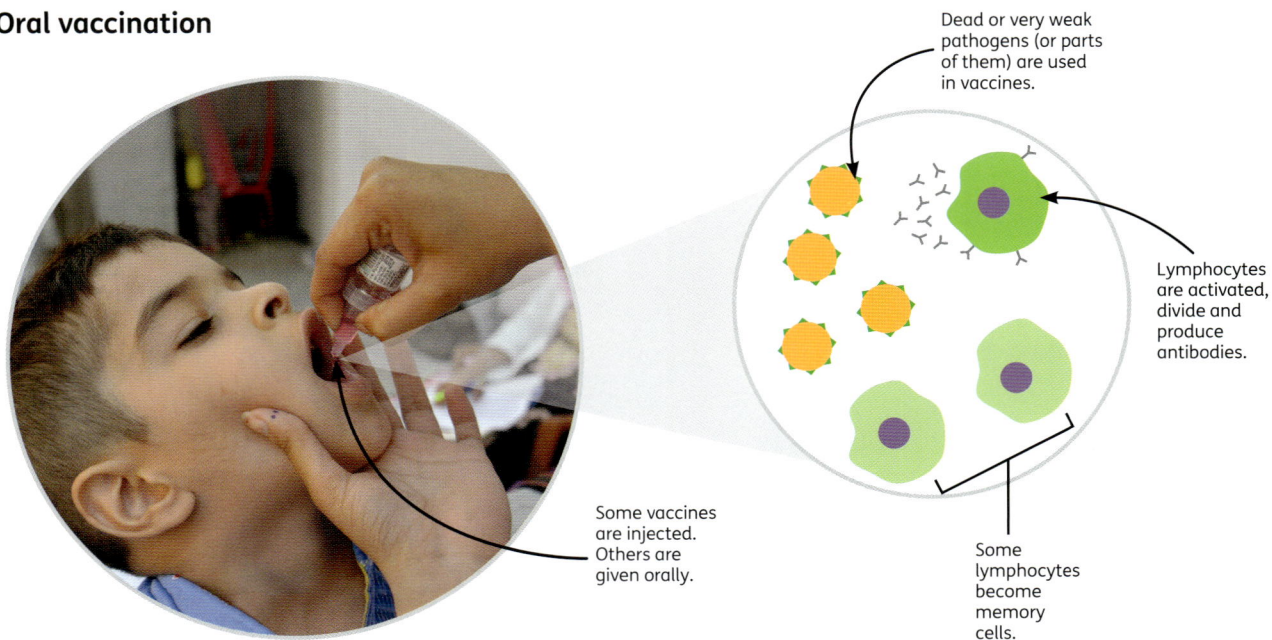

Antibiotics and Drug Development

Key terms

- Antibiotic
- Antiseptic
- Aseptic technique
- Bias
- Double-blind trial
- Placebo

Key facts

- Painkillers don't kill pathogens – they just ease disease symptoms.
- Antibiotics kill bacteria. Each antibiotic targets specific bacteria, so doctors must pick the right one.
- Antibiotics are safe inside our bodies because they only stop bacterial cell processes.
- Antiseptics are harsh chemicals that kill bacteria and are unsafe inside our bodies.

Drug origins

Traditionally, medicines were extracted from plants and microorganisms, for example:

- Penicillin (the first antibiotic, discovered by Alexander Fleming) comes from *Penicillium* mould.
- Digitalis (a heart drug) comes from foxgloves.
- Aspirin (a painkiller) comes from willow trees.

Scientists continue to look for drugs in plants.

Science skills

- A nutrient agar plate is spread with bacteria.
- Paper discs containing antibiotics are added.
- The plate is incubated in a warm place for 48 hours.
- Bacteria do not grow in the areas where an effective antibiotic is present.
- The bigger the inhibition zone, the more effective the antibiotic. Its area = πr^2 (where r is radius).

In these experiments, **aseptic techniques** are important. All materials for growing and handling bacteria are sterilised in an autoclave, and everything is kept covered.

Results

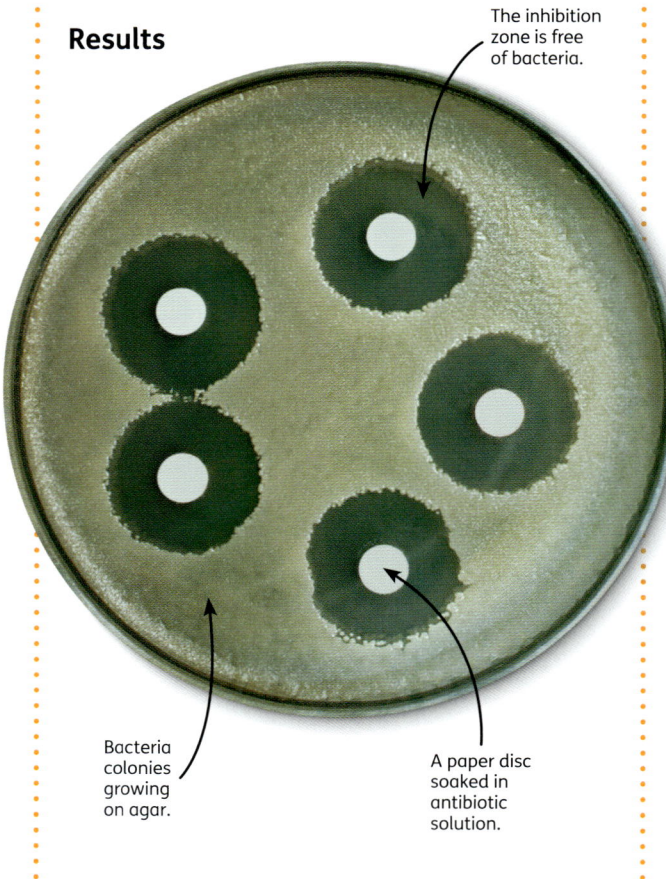

The inhibition zone is free of bacteria.

Bacteria colonies growing on agar.

A paper disc soaked in antibiotic solution.

Infection and Response

Antibiotic resistance

Antibiotics have greatly reduced the number of deaths from bacterial diseases, but some bacteria have become "resistant". This happens when bacteria mutate and the antibiotic stops working (see pages 92–93).

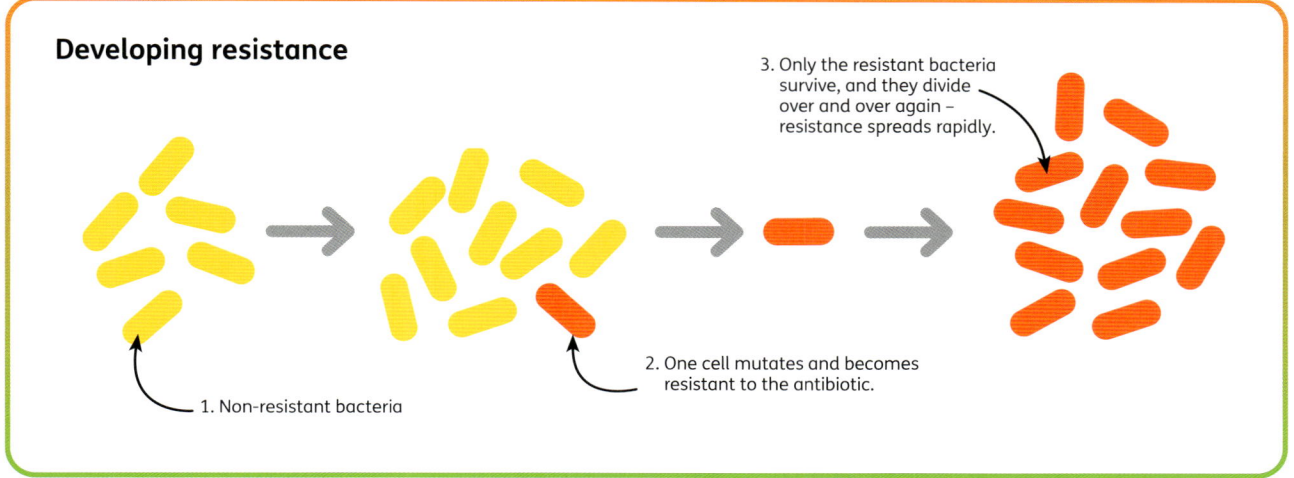

Developing resistance

1. Non-resistant bacteria
2. One cell mutates and becomes resistant to the antibiotic.
3. Only the resistant bacteria survive, and they divide over and over again – resistance spreads rapidly.

Drug development

- Pharmaceutical industry scientists screen millions of substances to find ones that kill pathogens.
- Trials ensure that substances are safe and work well in our bodies without harmful side effects.
- Viruses hide inside cells. So antiviral drugs are difficult to develop, because they can damage cells.
- In **double-blind trials**, some people take a **placebo** tablet. Nobody knows who is taking the placebo until the end. This reduces **bias**.

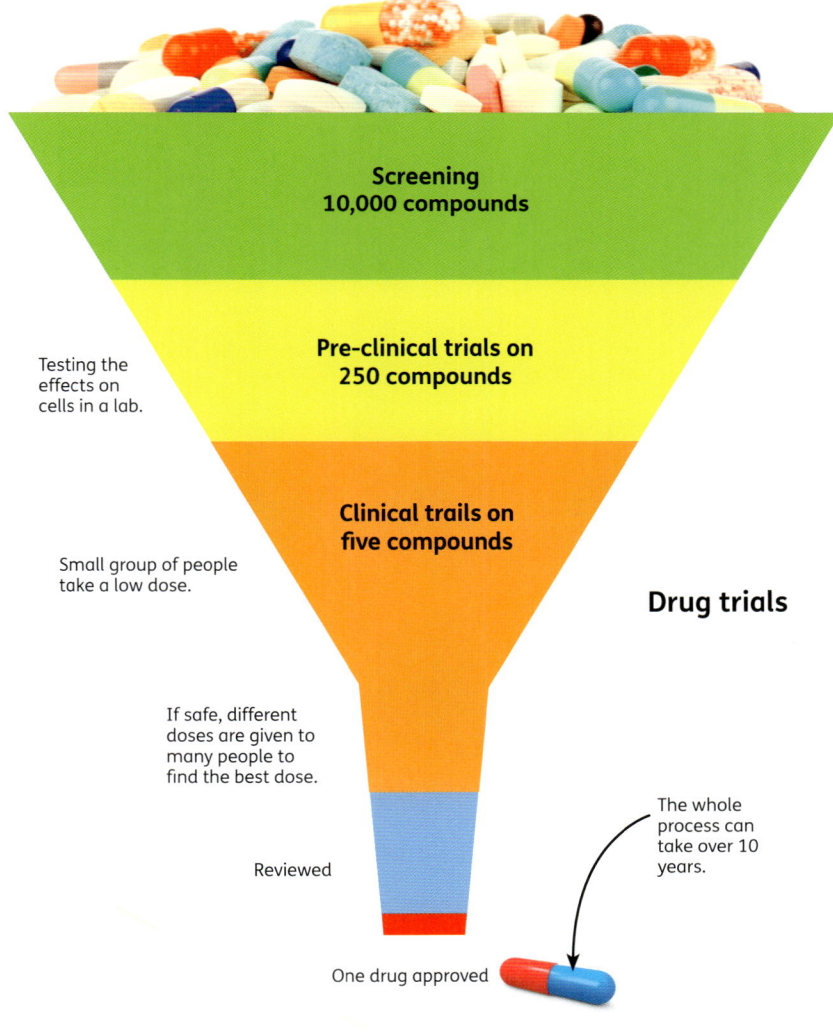

Screening 10,000 compounds

Pre-clinical trials on 250 compounds
Testing the effects on cells in a lab.

Clinical trails on five compounds
Small group of people take a low dose.

Drug trials

If safe, different doses are given to many people to find the best dose.

Reviewed

One drug approved

The whole process can take over 10 years.

Plant Diseases and Defences

Key terms
- Aphid
- Chalara ash dieback
- Rose black spot
- Tobacco Mosaic Virus (TMV)

Plants can be infected by viral, bacterial and fungal pathogens. Insect pests and lack of ions also make them unhealthy.

Plant diseases

Disease	Pathogen	Typical symptoms	Spread	Prevention
Rose black spot	Fungus	Black/purple spots on leaves, which turn yellow and drop. Reduces photosynthesis → stunted growth	Spores in water droplets (produced by rain splashes)	Remove and destroy infected leaves, use fungicides.
Chalara ash dieback	Fungus	Leaf loss, black patches on bark	Airborne spores	Remove and destroy infected trees.
Tobacco Mosaic Virus (TMV)	Fungus	Leaves, of tomatoes for example, develop a mosaic pattern of discolouration. Reduces photosynthesis → stunted growth	Contact between plants, contaminated tools	Remove and destroy infected plants, wash tools.

Other plant problems

- **Aphids** suck sugary sap from plant phloem.
  - Problem: Weaken the plant and can infect it with viruses.
  - Treatment: Use natural aphid predators, insecticides.

- **Lack of ions**
  - Problems: Lack of nitrogen causes stunted growth, lack of magnesium causes yellow leaves (chlorosis).
  - Treatment: Artificial fertilisers containing those ions.

Infection and Response

Plant defences

Plants defend themselves from pathogens and pests using chemical substances, physical barriers and mechanical deterrents.

Defence	Type	How it works
Cellulose cell walls	Physical	Barriers around cells
Tough waxy cuticle layer	Physical	Barrier covering leaves
Layers of dead cells around stems (for example tree bark)	Physical	Barrier, which removes pathogens when layers fall off
Antibacterial compounds	Chemical	Kill bacteria

Poisons
Chemical: Animals learn not to eat plants containing poisons or bitter-tasting substances. Humans use some of these for medicinal use. The poison in foxgloves (digitalis) is a heart medicine and bitter-tasting aspirin from willow tree bark is a painkiller.

Foxglove

Thorns and hairs
Mechanical: These keep all animals away.

Cactus

Leaves that curl
Mechanical: Curling leaves make a plant look unhealthy and less delicious to herbivores.

Leaflet
When touched, the leaflets start to fold.
The leaf droops and looks wilted.
Sensitive plant

Mimicry
Mechanical: Some plants have white blotches on their leaves, which look like bird droppings.

Lungwort

Brain Booster

Infection and Response Recap Quiz

 Find a pen and paper and work through these revision questions.

1. Complete the sentence with one word.
   Any microorganism that can cause a disease is described as a _____ .

2. Which of these diseases is caused by a protist? Choose one.
   gonorrhoea   measles   chalara   malaria

3. Give the name of the white blood cells that produce antibodies.

4. Give the name of the malaria vector.

5. State the function of lysozyme in tears.

6. Which of these ions are needed to make chlorophyll? Choose one.
   magnesium   nitrogen   potassium   calcium

7. Explain how vaccination prevents a disease.

8. Describe how tree bark acts as a plant defence.

9. At what point is a double-blind trial used when developing a new medicine? Choose one.
   screening   pre-clinical trial   clinical trial   review

10. Describe how measles is spread.

11. State how gonorrhoea can be treated.

12. Describe what happens during phagocytosis.

13. Which of these drugs is most suitable for treating Ebola? Choose one.
    antibiotic   aspirin   antiviral   digitalis

14. State one symptom of salmonella poisoning.

Check your answers on page **109**.

Bioenergetics

At the end of this chapter, you should be able to:

- ✓ Describe how a plant produces food by photosynthesis.
- ✓ Recall the word and chemical equations for photosynthesis.
- ✓ Explain how glucose is used in a plant.
- ✓ Define limiting factor.
- ✓ Explain how different factors affect the rate of photosynthesis.
- ✓ Describe how to investigate the rate of photosynthesis.
- ✓ Describe the process of respiration.
- ✓ Compare aerobic and anaerobic respiration.
- ✓ Compare anaerobic respiration in animals and other examples.
- ✓ Describe the changes that take place in the body during exercise.
- ✓ Define metabolism.

Bioenergetics

Photosynthesis

Key terms

- Endothermic reaction
- Producers
- Photosynthesis

Key facts

- Plants and algae are producers – they make their own food by photosynthesis.
- In photosynthesis, plants use light energy to combine carbon dioxide and water to make **glucose** and oxygen.
- Some of the oxygen is used in respiration. The rest is released as waste.

How photosynthesis occurs

5. Oxygen is released.

1. Sunlight provides the energy for photosynthesis. Plants use the light energy to convert carbon dioxide and water into glucose and oxygen.

Chloroplast

2. The leaves of a plant take in carbon dioxide from the air.

The cells in plants are packed with structures called chloroplasts. These contain the green pigment chlorophyll, which absorbs sunlight. Photosynthesis takes place inside the chloroplasts.

4. Water is absorbed from the soil through roots.

3. Minerals are taken in from the soil through roots. One of these minerals is magnesium, which is needed to make chlorophyll.

The root is covered in a layer of cells called the epidermis. Root hairs are long extensions of the epidermal cells. These hairs create a large surface area for absorbing water and minerals from the soil.

Bioenergetics 53

Photosynthesis reaction

Photosynthesis is an endothermic reaction – energy from the environment is taken in and transferred to the chloroplasts by light.

Photosynthesis involves many enzyme-controlled reactions. These take place in sequence and are represented by the equation:

$$6CO_2 + 6H_2O \xrightarrow[\text{chlorophyll}]{\text{sunlight}} C_6H_{12}O_6 + 6O_2$$

$$\text{carbon dioxide} + \text{water} \xrightarrow[\text{chlorophyll}]{\text{sunlight}} \text{glucose} + \text{oxygen}$$

RAPPING UP!

These are all the structures that you will see in plants.
Cell wall, vacuole and then the chloroplasts.
Pause this video so you can label the parts.
Photosynthesis is where we will make a start.

Takes in light and then CO_2.
Combines to water then makes food,
chlorophyll is where this brews.
Alongside glucose comes O_2.

Use of glucose

Some of the glucose a plant makes is used straightaway in respiration. To work, cells need energy, which is obtained from respiration. The rest is used in a number of other ways.

Sucrose is transported from leaves (the source) to roots.

Some of the glucose is used to make a complex sugar called sucrose. This is transported to parts of the plant that need it.

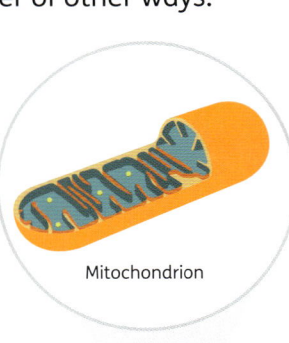

Mitochondrion

Tiny structures within a cell, called mitochondria (singular mitochondrion), transfer the energy stored in glucose to the cell during respiration.

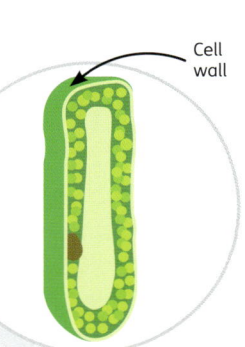

Cell wall

Cellulose, which is made from glucose, is needed to make cell walls. This gives the plant strength and support.

Fats and oils (known as lipids) are made from glucose. They are used as a food store and as a source of food for new seedlings.

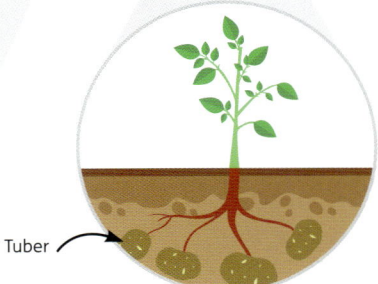

Tuber

The glucose that is not used straightaway is converted into starch. It is stored in the leaves, roots, and tubers for future use.

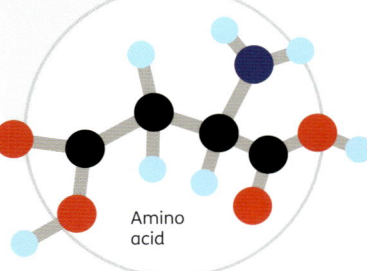

Amino acid

Amino acids form when glucose combines with nitrogen, which is absorbed as nitrates from the soil. Proteins are built from these amino acids and used for growth and cell repair.

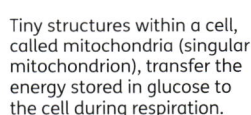

Bioenergetics

Rate of Photosynthesis

Key terms

- Chlorophyll
- Limiting factor

Key facts

- The rate of photosynthesis is affected by: temperature, light intensity, carbon dioxide concentration and the amount of chlorophyll.
- These are limiting factors – when any of these factors increase, they can make photosynthesis happen faster, but only up to a limit when photosynthesis works as fast as it can.
- Faster photosynthesis means a plant makes food more efficiently.

Light intensity

When light intensity increases, the rate of photosynthesis increases as more energy is transferred. However, it reaches a maximum level when photosynthesis cannot go any faster as another factor limits the reaction.

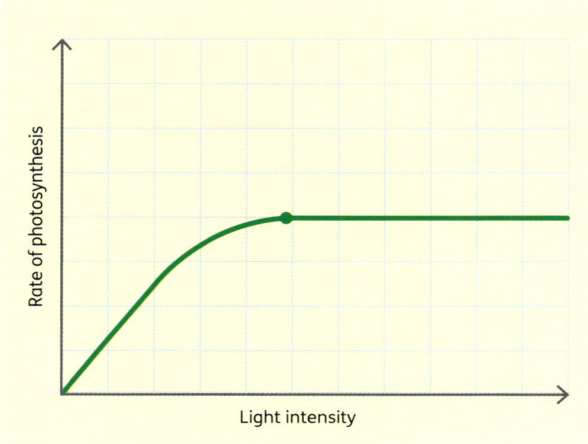

Temperature

When temperature increases, the molecules collide faster so the rate of photosynthesis increases. However, above the maximum rate, the enzymes used in photosynthesis denature (see page 27) and photosynthesis stops.

Carbon dioxide

When carbon dioxide concentration increases, the rate of photosynthesis increases as more carbon dioxide molecules collide with enzymes. However, it reaches a maximum level when photosynthesis cannot go any faster as another factor limits the reaction.

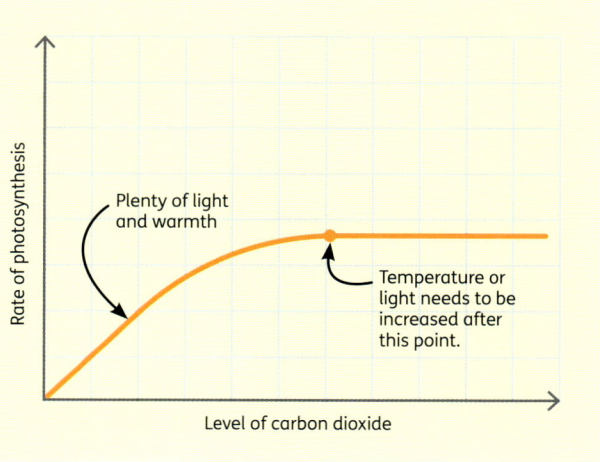

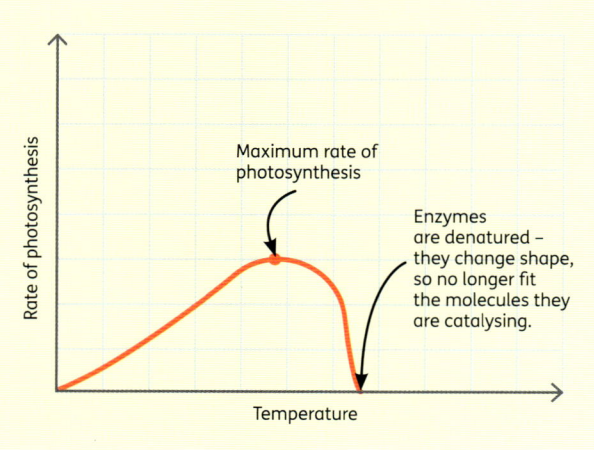

Bioenergetics

Amount of chlorophyll

The more **chlorophyll** a plant contains, the more light energy it can trap, and therefore the faster the rate of photosynthesis. This means that large leaves are more efficient than small leaves.

Plants with variegated leaves have patches where green chlorophyll is absent. These parts of the plant cannot photosynthesise. So, their overall rate of photosynthesis is likely to be lower than in a plant with all-green leaves, making them less efficient at making food.

Variegated leaf

Key facts

- Aquatic plants are often used to investigate the rate of photosynthesis.
- The rate of photosynthesis can be measured by:
  - Counting the bubbles of oxygen produced.
  - Using a gas syringe to determine the volume of oxygen produced.
- The more oxygen produced in a set amount of time, the faster the rate of photosynthesis.

Science skills

1. Place some pondweed (with the cut end at the top) in a test tube of sodium hydrogen carbonate solution. This releases carbon dioxide needed for photosynthesis.
2. Place the test tube in a beaker of water 10 cm from the light. This acts as a water bath to keep the temperature constant.
3. Leave the pondweed for 5 minutes.
4. Count how many bubbles are produced in 1 minute. Repeat two more times and calculate an average.

Repeat steps 3 and 4 at different distances from the light source.

$$\text{Rate of transpiration (bubbles/min)} = \frac{\text{Number of bubbles}}{\text{Time taken (in minutes)}}$$

Light source

The light intensity is the independent variable – you can change how close the light source is to the pondweed.

The number of oxygen bubbles produced is the dependent variable.

Water in the beaker insulates the plant in the tube, helping to stop the lamp from warming it up.

Ruler

The type of pondweed, temperature, and amount of sodium hydrogen carbonate are all controlled variables. They are kept the same so only the distance from the light source will affect the results.

Bioenergetics

Respiration, Exercise and Metabolism

Key terms

- Aerobic
- Anaerobic
- Exothermic reaction
- Fermentation
- Respiration

Key facts

- Respiration supplies all the energy needed for living processes.
- It takes place inside the mitochondria.
- It can take place aerobically (using oxygen) or anaerobically (without oxygen).
- Aerobic respiration transfers energy more efficiently than anaerobic respiration.

Uses of energy

Respiration is an exothermic reaction. Chemical reactions controlled by enzymes break down the chemical bonds in food molecules such as glucose, releasing energy to the cells.

Organisms need energy for all living processes. These include:

- Growth and repair.
- Movement.
- Keeping warm.

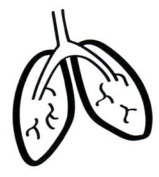

Anaerobic respiration

During anaerobic respiration, glucose is only partly broken down, so energy is released from each glucose molecule compared to aerobic respiration.

Anaerobic respiration can be used in special circumstances, such as to get a bigger burst of energy during strenuous exercise or when oxygen levels are low.

Anaerobic respiration in animals can be summarised by the equation:

$$C_6H_{12}O_6 \longrightarrow 2C_3H_6O_3$$
glucose $\longrightarrow$ lactic acid (+ energy)

Lactic acid builds up in muscle cells. This can make the muscles become fatigued (tired) and cause cramps.

Aerobic respiration

Most respiration occurs aerobically, when oxygen is present. Oxygen is taken into the body through the lungs.

It is summarised by the equation:

$$C_6H_{12}O_6 + 6O_2 \longrightarrow 6CO_2 + 6H_2O \text{ (+ energy)}$$

glucose + oxygen $\longrightarrow$ carbon dioxide + water (+ energy)

Water is used in the body or expelled as a waste product in sweat, tears, exhalation or urine. Carbon dioxide is lost when you breathe out.

Bioenergetics 57

Anaerobic respiration in other organisms

Anaerobic respiration produces different products in other organisms.

- Anaerobic respiration in yeast is used for making bread and alcoholic drinks through a process called fermentation.
- In waterlogged soil, the amount of oxygen available for plant root cells is reduced and so they have to respire anaerobically, producing carbon dioxide and ethanol.

Anaerobic respiration in plant and yeast cells is represented by the equation:

$$C_6H_{12}O_6 \rightarrow 2C_2H_5OH + 2CO_2$$

glucose $\rightarrow$ ethanol + carbon dioxide (+ energy)

Metabolism is the sum of all the reactions in a cell or the body.
These reactions build up molecules and break them down.
They are controlled by enzymes.
Some reactions:

- Release energy, such as respiration.
- Take in energy, such as formation of lipids from glycerol and fatty acids. Respiration transfers the energy for these reactions.

Exercise

During exercise, muscle cells must carry out more aerobic respiration, so:

- Breathing rate and depth increase – this allows more oxygen to be taken into the body (and more carbon dioxide to be removed).
- The heart beats faster to pump blood around the body quicker, delivering more oxygen to the muscles.

However, soon, the heart and lungs are working as fast as they can. Extra energy then comes from anaerobic respiration. This doesn't need any more oxygen, but does causes a build up of lactic acid and creates an oxygen debt.

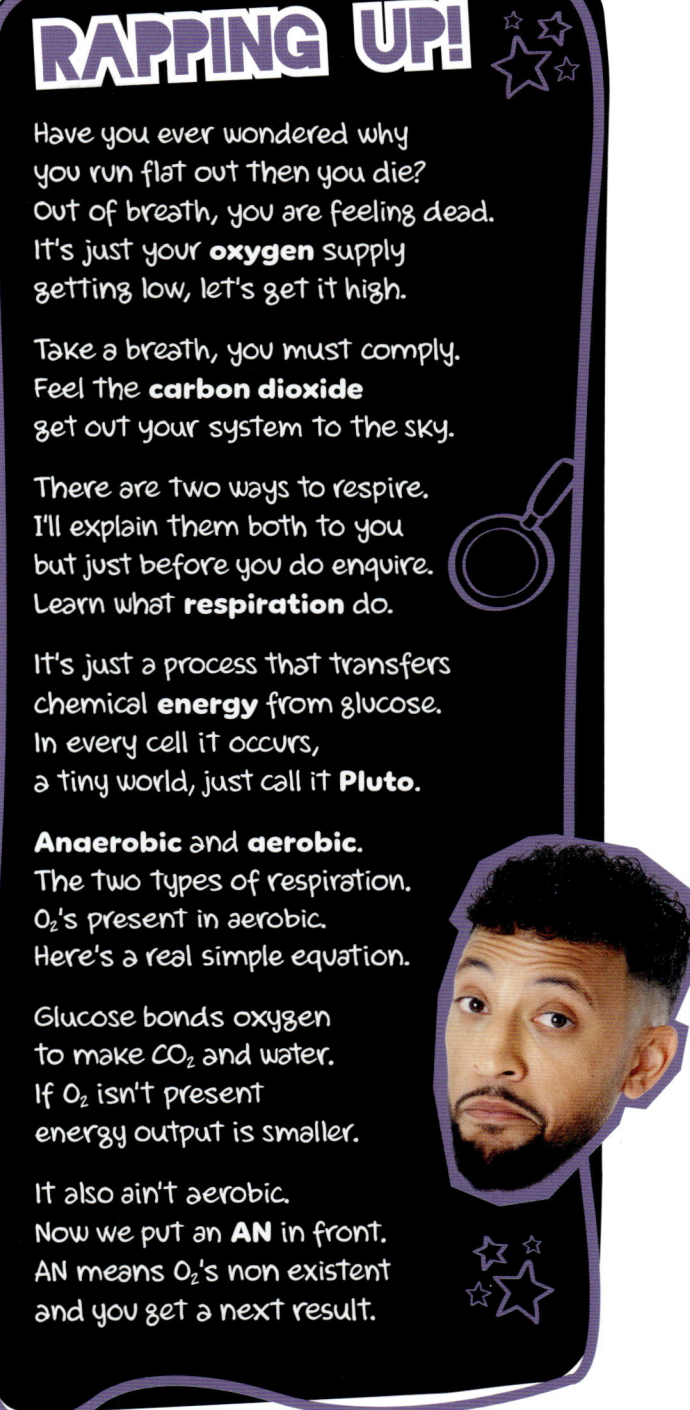

RAPPING UP!

Have you ever wondered why
you run flat out then you die?
Out of breath, you are feeling dead.
It's just your **oxygen** supply
getting low, let's get it high.

Take a breath, you must comply.
Feel the **carbon dioxide**
get out your system to the sky.

There are two ways to respire.
I'll explain them both to you
but just before you do enquire.
Learn what **respiration** do.

It's just a process that transfers
chemical **energy** from glucose.
In every cell it occurs,
a tiny world, just call it **Pluto**.

Anaerobic and **aerobic**.
The two types of respiration.
O_2's present in aerobic.
Here's a real simple equation.

Glucose bonds oxygen
to make CO_2 and water.
If O_2 isn't present
energy output is smaller.

It also ain't aerobic.
Now we put an **AN** in front.
AN means O_2's non existent
and you get a next result.

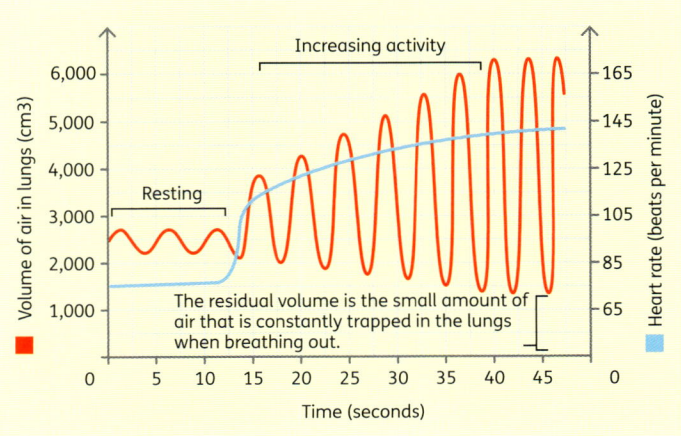

Brain Booster

Bioenergetics Recap Quiz

 Find a pen and paper and work through these revision questions.

1. Where in the cell does respiration take place?
   chloroplast   mitochondria   vacuole

2. Give **two** uses of glucose in a plant.

3. Complete the word equation for photosynthesis.
   water + _____ → glucose + _____

4. Select the correct chemical formula for glucose.
   $C_6H_{12}O_6$ $6CO_{26}$ $2C_3H_6O_3$

5. State one way the rate of photosynthesis can be measured using an aquatic plant.

6. Which of the following temperatures would cause the greatest rate of photosynthesis?
   a) 20°C   35°C   50°C
   b) Give a reason for your answer.

7. Give **two** reasons why the body normally respires aerobically.

8. Explain why heart rate and breathing rate increase during exercise.

9. Give one commercial use of fermentation.

10. Define metabolism.

Check your answers on pages **109–110**.

Homeostasis and Response

At the end of this chapter, you should be able to:

- ✓ Explain how the nervous system helps to coordinate actions.
- ✓ Identify parts of the brain and describe their functions.
- ✓ Identify the parts of the eye and describe their functions.
- ✓ Explain why homeostasis is important.
- ✓ Describe the control of blood glucose and water.
- ✓ Explain how hormones help to regulate body functions, including their role in reproduction.
- ✓ Explain methods of contraception, including the use of hormones.
- ✓ Describe the effects of plant hormones.

Homeostasis and the Nervous System

Homeostasis is your body keeping the conditions inside you just right so that everything works well. Examples include: the control of blood glucose levels, water levels and body temperature.

Key terms

- Coordinator
- Effector
- Homeostasis
- Motor neurone
- Receptor
- Reflex arc
- Relay neurone
- Response
- Sensory neurone
- Stimulus

Control systems

In all control systems:

- **Stimuli** (changes in the environment) are detected by…
- **Receptors**, which transfer information to…
- **Coordinators** (for example, brain, spinal cord, pancreas), which process the information and cause…
- **Effectors** (for example, muscle, gland) to produce a…
- **Response**, which adjusts levels to keep them just right.

Types of neurone

Cell body — Axon — Dendrite

Sensory neurones detect stimuli, such as light, and send electrical impulses to the CNS.

Cell body

Dendrite — Axon — Cell body

Relay neurones pass on signals from sensory neurones to motor neurones.

Motor neurones carry signals from the CNS to effector organs.

Nervous system

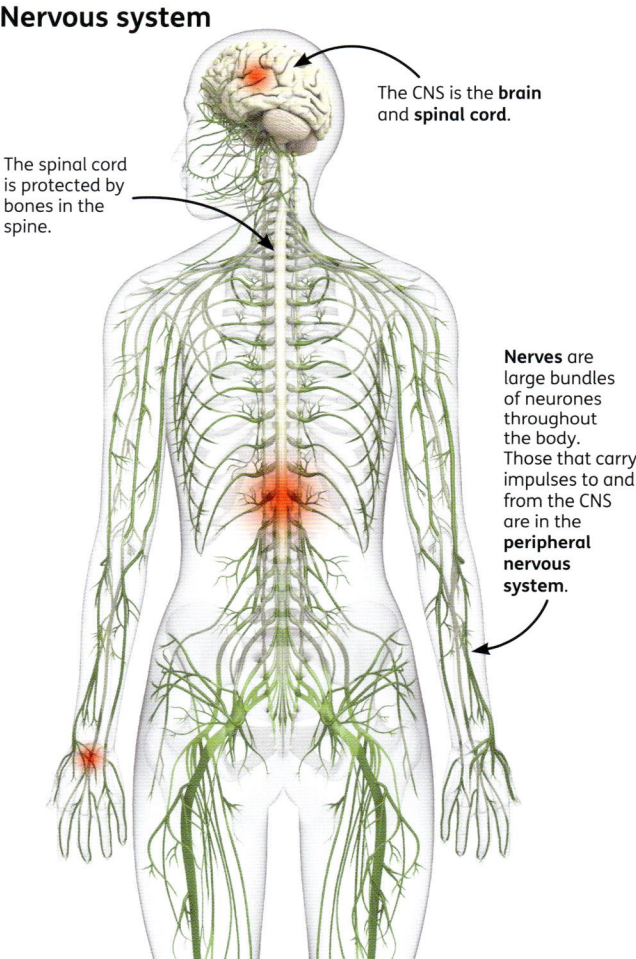

The CNS is the **brain** and **spinal cord**.

The spinal cord is protected by bones in the spine.

Nerves are large bundles of neurones throughout the body. Those that carry impulses to and from the CNS are in the **peripheral nervous system**.

Receptors in the body send information using electrical impulses, which travel along **neurones** to the central nervous system (CNS). The CNS coordinates a response by sending impulses along neurones to effectors.

Homeostasis and Response 61

Reflex actions

These actions are super-fast, automatic responses that protect you. They don't involve the thinking part of the brain, so they happen in a flash. A reflex action uses a set of neurones in a **reflex arc**.

The pain reflex
The withdrawal reflex quickly pulls part of the body away from a pain stimulus.

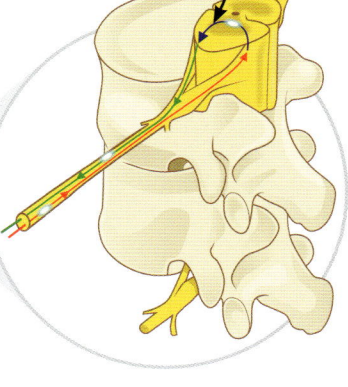

1. **Stimulus**
A thorn on the cactus pierces the skin. This is the stimulus.

2. **Receptor**
Receptor cells in the skin detect the stimulus. This causes an impulse to travel along the sensory neurone to the spinal cord.

3. **Spinal cord**
A relay neurone in the spinal cord receives the impulse and sends an impulse to a motor neurone.

4. **Effector**
The motor neurone sends a nerve impulse to a muscle in the arm (the effector), which then contracts, pulling the hand away from the source of pain.

RAPPING UP!

They're two parts to the nervous system:
this one's central, this one's different.
Central is brain and spinal cord;
peripheral is there to connect your CNS
to the rest of your body.

Do these nerves, then list them properly:
sensory **neurones** send impulses
from the receptors they're repulsive.
That then goes to the CNS.
Sensory done, let me list the rest.

Number two is the motor neurone;
takes that pulse to a **cause and effect**.
Usually a muscle or could be a gland
gets impulsed and delivers the plan.

You on three it's time don't play,
its name is called relay.

Now it's time for the best part:
we call this the reflex arc.
It's there to **protect** us from pain.
Happens so quick it bypasses the brain.

Stimulus comes, let's say a bee,
triggers the **receptors** underneath.
Sensory neurone, this thing goes
sends to the relay – it's one of those.

After the relay onto the **motor**,
gives you a twist and don't play poker.
Then onto the **effector**
the response that comes – is to protect ya.

The Brain and Temperature Control

Key terms

- Cerebellum
- Cerebral cortex
- Hypothalamus
- Medulla
- Thermoregulation
- Vasoconstriction
- Vasodilation

Your brain is made up of billions of interconnected neurones communicating to control functions including conscious thought, memory and language.

Different brain regions have different functions

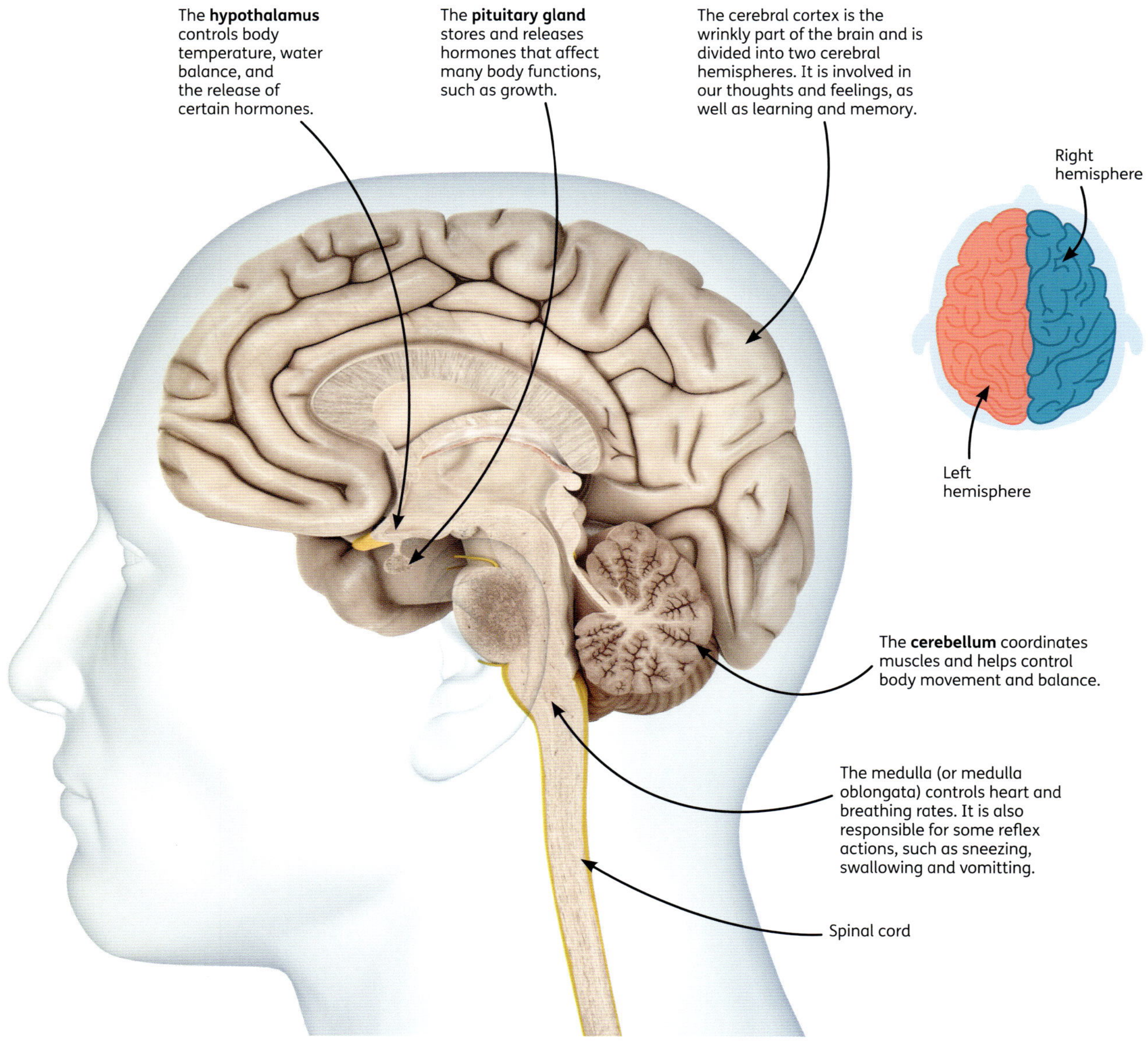

The **hypothalamus** controls body temperature, water balance, and the release of certain hormones.

The **pituitary gland** stores and releases hormones that affect many body functions, such as growth.

The cerebral cortex is the wrinkly part of the brain and is divided into two cerebral hemispheres. It is involved in our thoughts and feelings, as well as learning and memory.

Right hemisphere

Left hemisphere

The **cerebellum** coordinates muscles and helps control body movement and balance.

The medulla (or medulla oblongata) controls heart and breathing rates. It is also responsible for some reflex actions, such as sneezing, swallowing and vomiting.

Spinal cord

Homeostasis and Response 63

Key facts

- Your internal temperature is kept at about 37°C by **thermoregulation**. This is important for keeping enzymes working efficiently – too hot or cold and they don't work so well (see pages 26–27).
- Receptors in the thermoregulatory centre in the hypothalamus detect blood temperature changes.
- Temperature receptors in the **dermis** also send nerve impulses to this centre.
- If body temperature is too low → shivering of skeletal muscles + vasoconstriction (dermis blood vessels become narrow).
- If body temperature is too high sweating **vasodilation**.

RAPPING UP!

Look, there are three parts of the **brain**.
Inside your skull is where they're contained.
Cortex, cerebellum, medulla.
Learn their jobs, remember their names.

This deals with high-level responses.
It's the cortex, it's where your **conscious, language, memory and your intelligence**,
two halves – that part's not irrelevant.

Cerebellum controls your **balance**.
Coordination now that's its talent.
For tasks you don't think about,
like when you walk or use your mouth.

Moving on, now the **medulla**.
White and grey are its two colours.
Keeps your unconscious mind straight,
just like your heart and breathing rate.

Next part here, it ain't that glamorous.
We call it the **hypothalamus**.
It controls your water levels
and temperature in your blood vessels.

Last part here, you have to respect
as without it we would be dead.
You might have guessed, it's the **reflex**.
Tap right there, and watch the knee flex.

The role of the skin

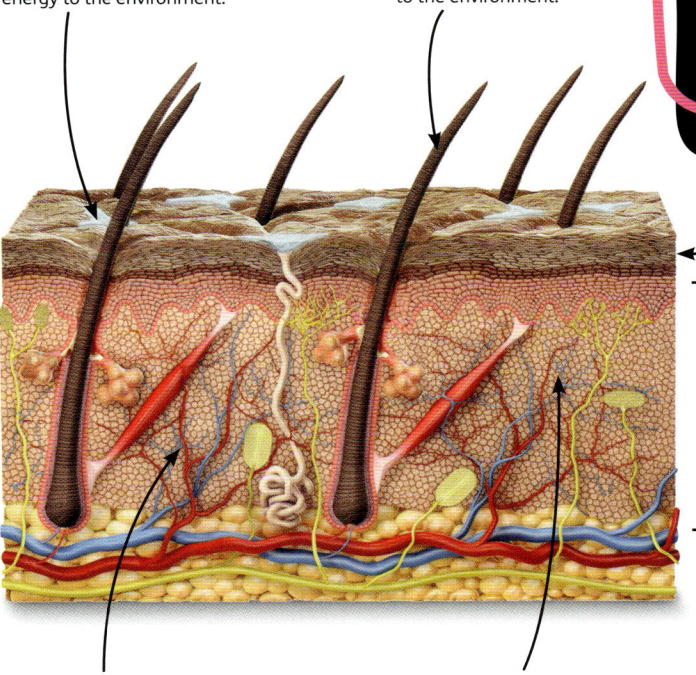

Temperature too high – glands release sweat, which evaporates from the **epidermis**, transferring energy to the environment.

Temperature too low – hairs stand up to trap air for insulation and reduce energy transfer to the environment.

Temperature too high – vasoconstriction allows less blood to flow to the skin surface.

Temperature too low – vasodilation allows more blood to flow to the skin surface, so more energy is transferred to the environment.

Epidermis

Dermis

Homeostasis and Response

The Eye

Adaptation to light conditions

The eye is a sense organ that contains receptors (rods and cones) that detect changes in light intensity and colour. These cells are protected from bright light by the iris muscles making the pupil small. In dim light, the iris muscles allow the pupil to dilate and let in more light.

Key terms

- Accommodation
- Ciliary muscles
- Cornea
- Iris
- Lens
- Myopia
- Optic nerve
- Pupil
- Retina
- Sclera

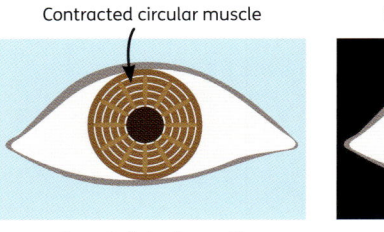

Constricted pupil   **Dilated pupil**

Eye structure

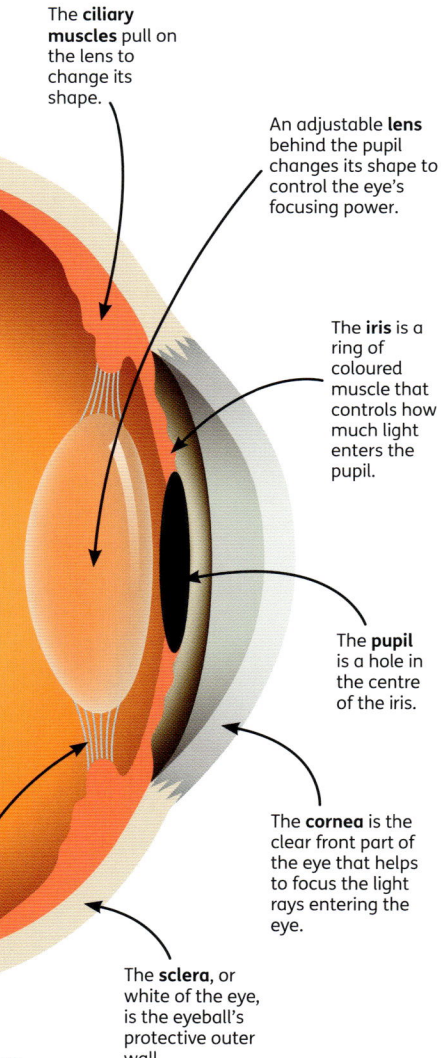

The **ciliary muscles** pull on the lens to change its shape.

An adjustable **lens** behind the pupil changes its shape to control the eye's focusing power.

The **iris** is a ring of coloured muscle that controls how much light enters the pupil.

The **pupil** is a hole in the centre of the iris.

The **cornea** is the clear front part of the eye that helps to focus the light rays entering the eye.

The **sclera**, or white of the eye, is the eyeball's protective outer wall.

The **optic nerve** carries nerve impulses to the brain.

The **retina** is a layer of light-sensitive receptor cells inside the eye. Cells called cones, concentrated in the centre of the retina, detect colours. Cells called rods are sensitive to faint light, but can't detect colour.

The **suspensory ligaments** hold the lens in place and connect it to the ciliary muscles.

Homeostasis and Response 65

Accommodation
Accommodation is when the shape of the lens changes to focus on near objects or distant ones.

Near vision
To focus on near objects:
- Ciliary muscles contract.
- Suspensory ligaments loosen.
- The lens becomes thicker.
- Strongly refracts light rays.

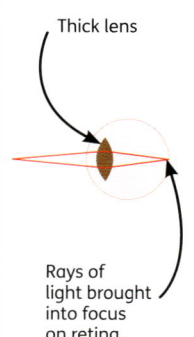

Thick lens

Rays of light brought into focus on retina.

Near vision

Far vision
To focus on distant objects:
- Ciliary muscles relax.
- Suspensory ligaments are pulled tight.
- The lens becomes thinner.
- Light rays not refracted as much.

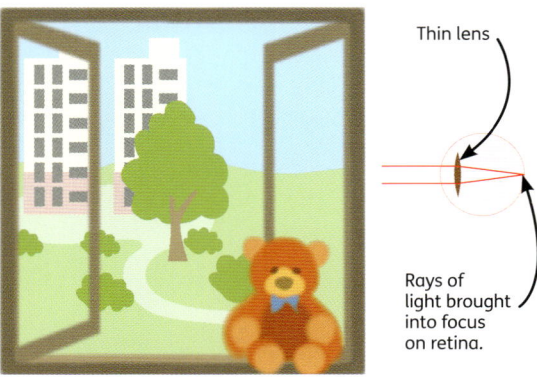

Thin lens

Rays of light brought into focus on retina.

Far vision

Eye problems

- **Colour blindness**: some cones do not work well and make it difficult to see some colours. This cannot be corrected.
- **Cataracts**: proteins make the lens go cloudy. Corrected by replacing the lens with a plastic one.
- **Hyperopia (long-sightedness)**: light rays focus behind the retina. Corrected by a convex lens, lens replacement or laser surgery to reshape the cornea.
- **Myopia (short-sightedness)**: light rays focus in front of the retina. Corrected by a concave lens, lens replacement or laser surgery.

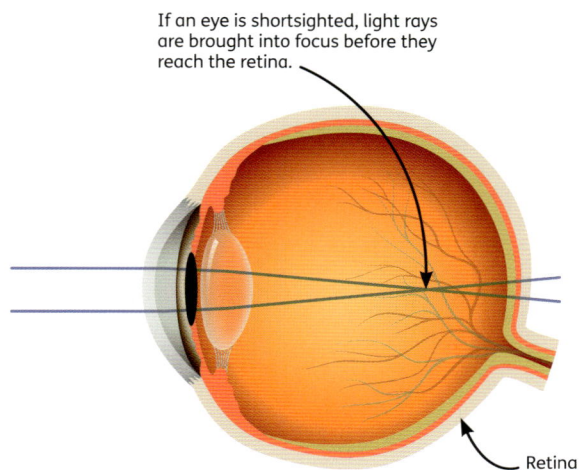

If an eye is shortsighted, light rays are brought into focus before they reach the retina.

Retina

Shortsighted eye

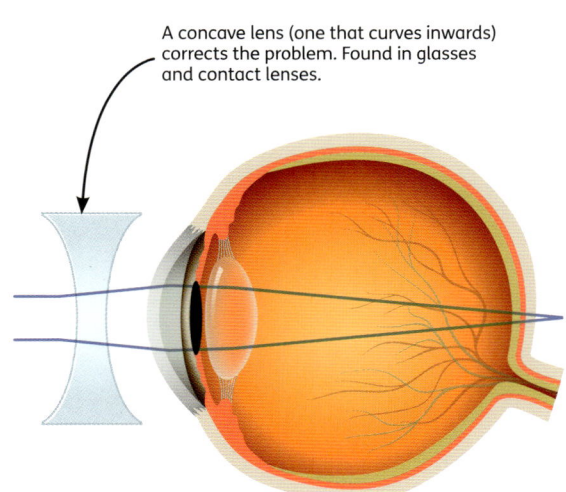

A concave lens (one that curves inwards) corrects the problem. Found in glasses and contact lenses.

Corrected vision

Homeostasis and Response

The Endocrine System

Key terms

- Adrenal gland
- Endocrine gland
- Endocrine system
- Hormone
- Ovaries
- Pancreas
- Pituitary gland
- Target organ
- Testes
- Thyroid

The endocrine system is made up of endocrine glands that secrete chemical hormones into the blood. Hormones control many processes. They're the reason you grow, sleep, get stressed and crave snacks.

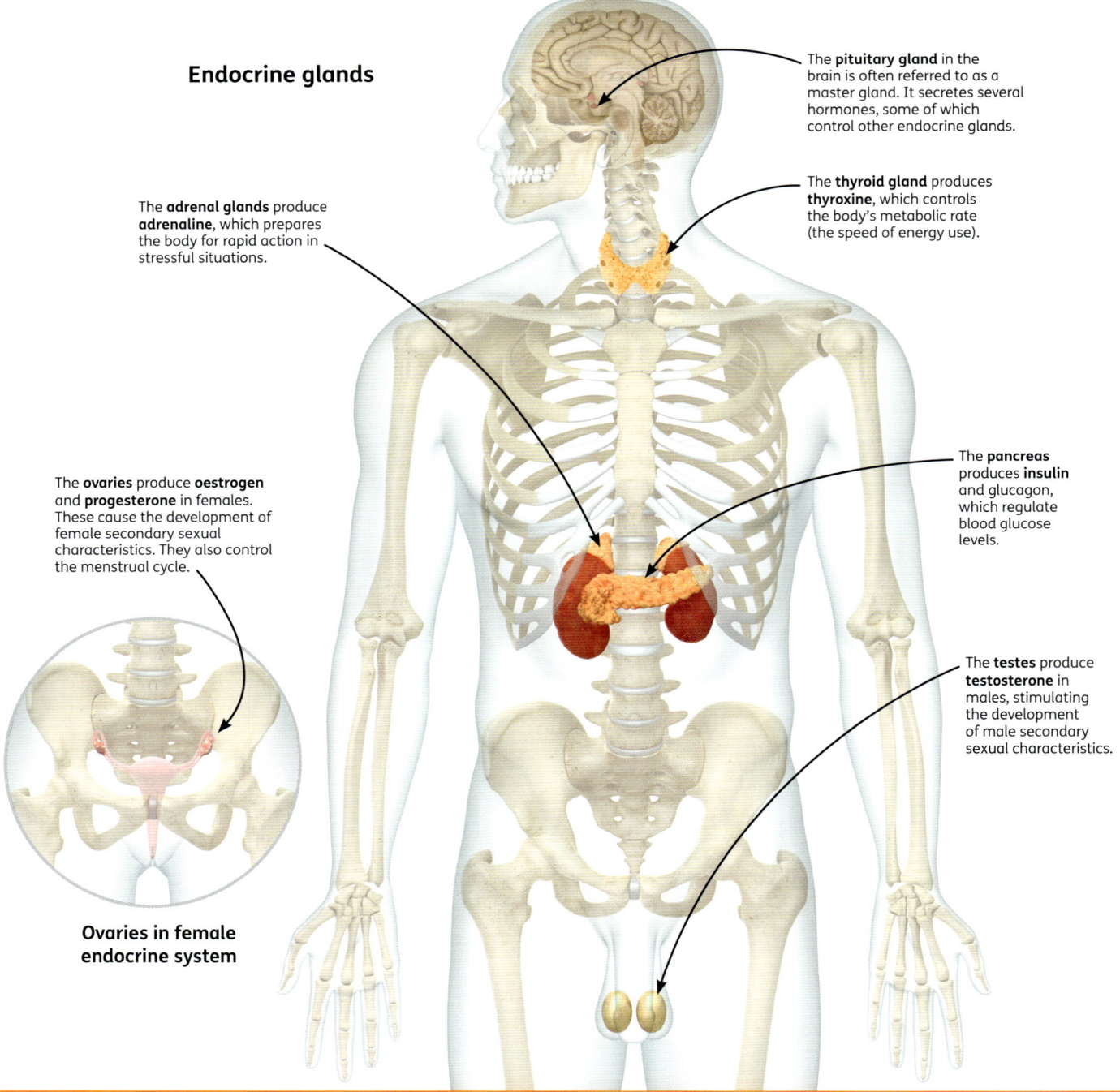

Endocrine glands

The **pituitary gland** in the brain is often referred to as a master gland. It secretes several hormones, some of which control other endocrine glands.

The **thyroid gland** produces **thyroxine**, which controls the body's metabolic rate (the speed of energy use).

The **adrenal glands** produce **adrenaline**, which prepares the body for rapid action in stressful situations.

The **pancreas** produces **insulin** and glucagon, which regulate blood glucose levels.

The **ovaries** produce **oestrogen** and **progesterone** in females. These cause the development of female secondary sexual characteristics. They also control the menstrual cycle.

The **testes** produce **testosterone** in males, stimulating the development of male secondary sexual characteristics.

Ovaries in female endocrine system

Homeostasis and Response

Fear response

When a cat is scared its nervous system goes into full panic mode and causes its fur to stand up. The adrenal glands also release adrenaline, increasing the breathing and heart rates. This prepares the cat for "fight or flight". When the "danger" has passed, the fur settles quickly but the heart and breathing rates remain high for longer.

Key facts

- When target organs detect hormones in the blood, they change their activity.
- Hormones are slower to cause responses in their target organs than nervous impulses.
- The effects of hormones last longer and affect a greater number of body parts than nervous system responses.

A cat's fur stands on end when it's frightened.

Science skills

Scientific theories change over time as new discoveries are made, for example:

- When food enters the small intestine, it is the stimulus for digestive enzymes to be released.
- Scientists once thought that all responses were controlled by the nervous system.
- In 1902, some scientists showed that digestive enzymes were released when the nerves were not working.
- Their hypothesis was that intestine receptor cells released a chemical that triggered enzyme release.
- Many experiments since have provided evidence to support this hypothesis, and it has become a theory.

RAPPING UP!

I hope you understand.
Looking over **hormones** is the plan.
They might travel in the body through the **bloodstream**
but they're released by the glands.
I'll expand.
It's the target organ where they land.
For example, we got **oestrogen** for ladies;
it's **testosterone** for man.
Slow mo, slow mo, everybody slow mo.
Nerves act quick but hormones not so.
Nerves electric and hormones blood flow.
I'll give you more examples down below.
Adrenaline released when it's time you go,
insulin controls all your blood glucose.
Your **thyroid** produces what I call thyro,
makes metabolism go fast or slow.

Homeostasis and Response

Control of Blood Glucose

Key terms
- Diabetes
- Glycogen
- Insulin
- Obesity
- Pancreas
- Risk factor

Key facts
- The pancreas contains receptor cells for blood glucose levels.
- The pancreas secretes two hormones:
  - Insulin lowers glucose levels.
  - Glucagon increases them.

Keeping an eye on your blood is ery important. It has to be just right. If blood glucose concentration is too high, it damages blood vessels, nerves and organs. Too low, and your cells run out of fuel.

Action of insulin and glucagon

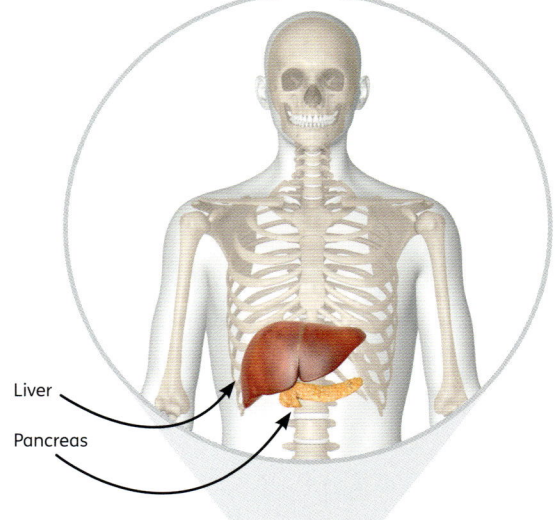

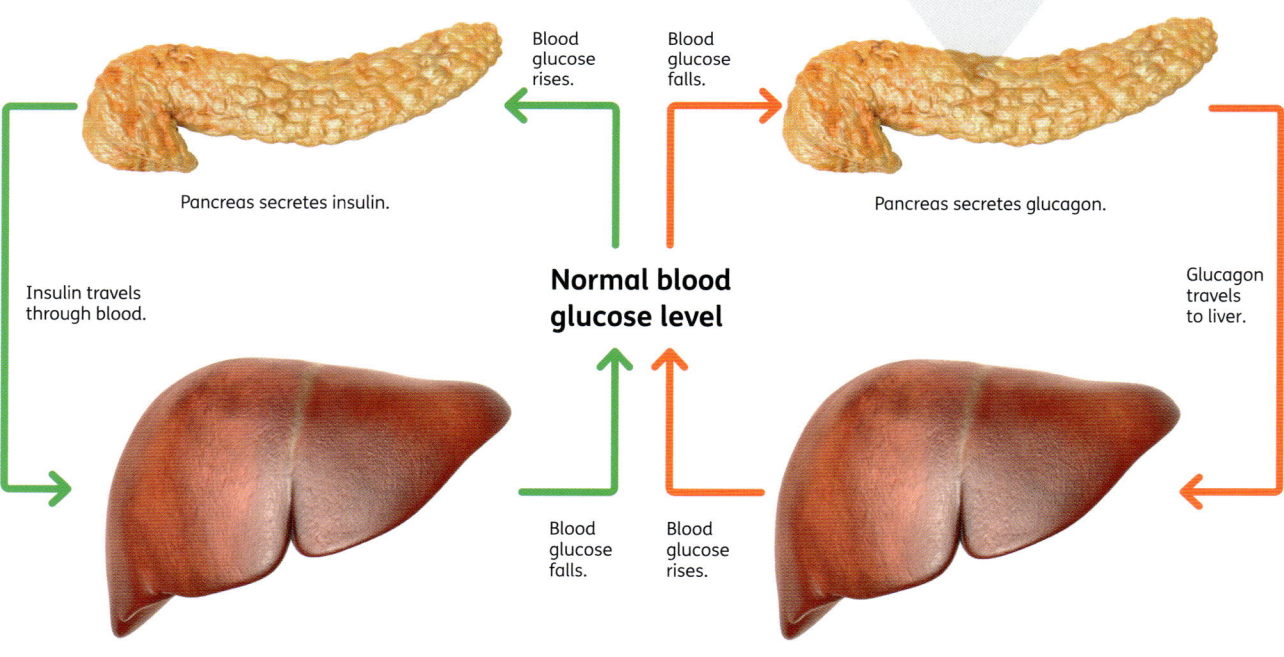

Blood glucose rises. — Pancreas secretes insulin. — Insulin travels through blood. — Liver converts glucose to glycogen and body cells take up glucose. — Blood glucose falls. — **Normal blood glucose level** — Blood glucose rises. — Liver converts glycogen to glucose. — Glucagon travels to liver. — Pancreas secretes glucagon. — Blood glucose falls.

Homeostasis and Response

Diabetes

Diabetes is a medical condition in which the body's blood glucose control system stops working properly. There are two types of diabetes: Type 1 and Type 2.

	Type 1 Diabetes	Type 2 Diabetes
Onset	Young age	Later in life
Cause	Pancreas does not produce insulin.	Body cells do not respond to insulin.
Usual treatment	Insulin injections	Avoid sugary foods and drinks, do exercise.
Prevention	No	Eat well and exercise. Obesity is a risk factor (see page 32).

Blood glucose levels

Blood glucose levels rise after eating and should quickly return to normal. However, glucose levels can stay high in people with Type 1 diabetes. To prevent this, diabetics inject themselves with insulin about 30 minutes before eating.

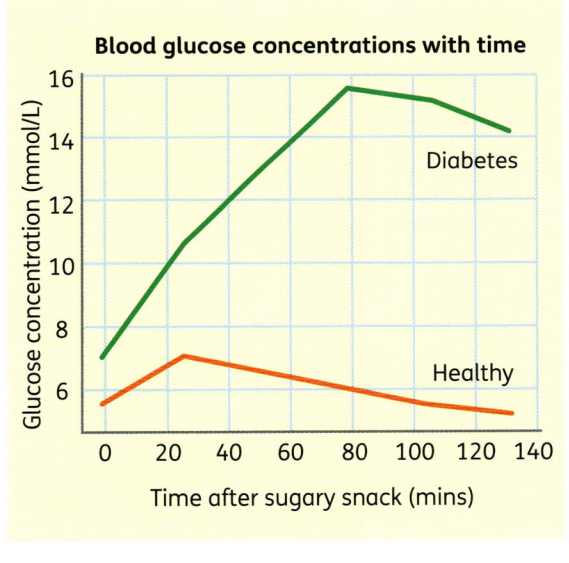

Type 2 risk factors

- A **risk factor** increases the chance of something.
- **Obesity** is a risk factor for Type 2 diabetes.
- Obesity is a Body Mass Index (BMI) > 30.

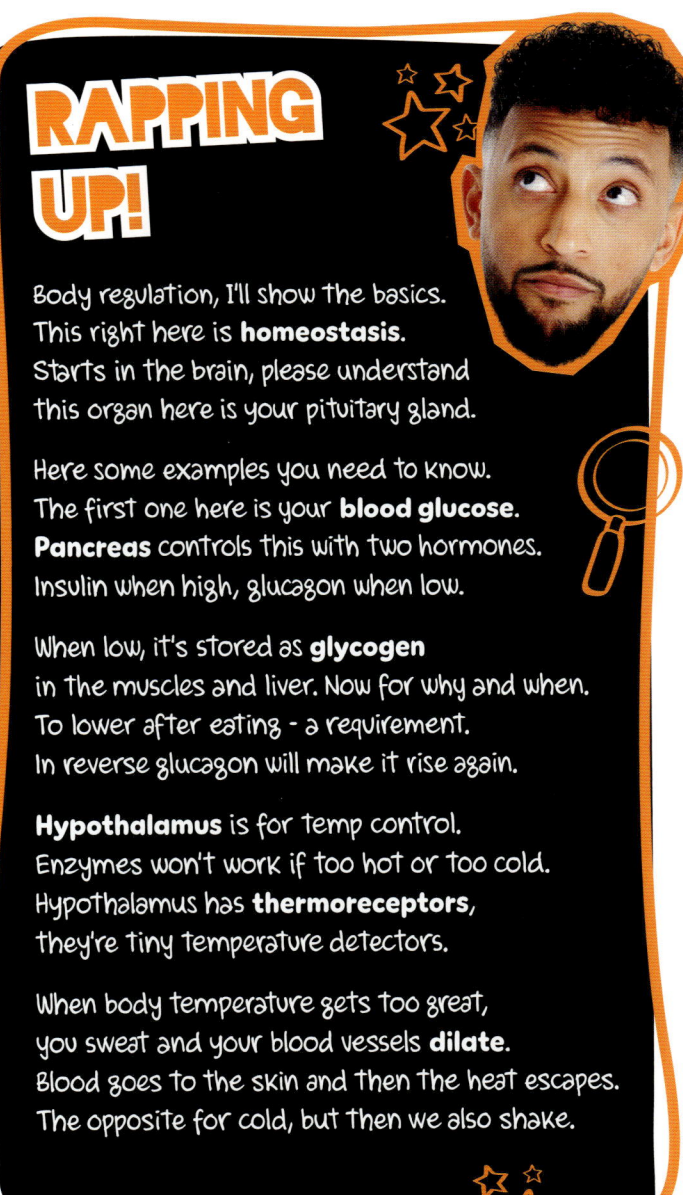

RAPPING UP!

Body regulation, I'll show the basics.
This right here is **homeostasis**.
Starts in the brain, please understand
this organ here is your pituitary gland.

Here some examples you need to know.
The first one here is your **blood glucose**.
Pancreas controls this with two hormones.
Insulin when high, glucagon when low.

When low, it's stored as **glycogen**
in the muscles and liver. Now for why and when.
To lower after eating - a requirement.
In reverse glucagon will make it rise again.

Hypothalamus is for temp control.
Enzymes won't work if too hot or too cold.
Hypothalamus has **thermoreceptors**,
they're tiny temperature detectors.

When body temperature gets too great,
you sweat and your blood vessels **dilate**.
Blood goes to the skin and then the heat escapes.
The opposite for cold, but then we also shake.

Homeostasis and Response

Water Balance

Key terms

- Dialysis
- Kidney
- Urea
- Urine
- Water balance

Key facts

Water enters and leaves cells by osmosis.
- Cells swell and can burst if they gain too much water.
- Cells shrink and do not work properly if they lose too much water.
- Maintaining the correct water balance is an example of homeostasis.

Gain and loss

- Water is gained from food and drink.
- Water is lost by:
  - Exhalation.
  - Sweating (along with ions and urea).
  - **Urine** (made in the **kidneys**).

Water level receptors in the brain control the release of the hormone ADH. This hormone alters the amount of water lost in the urine.

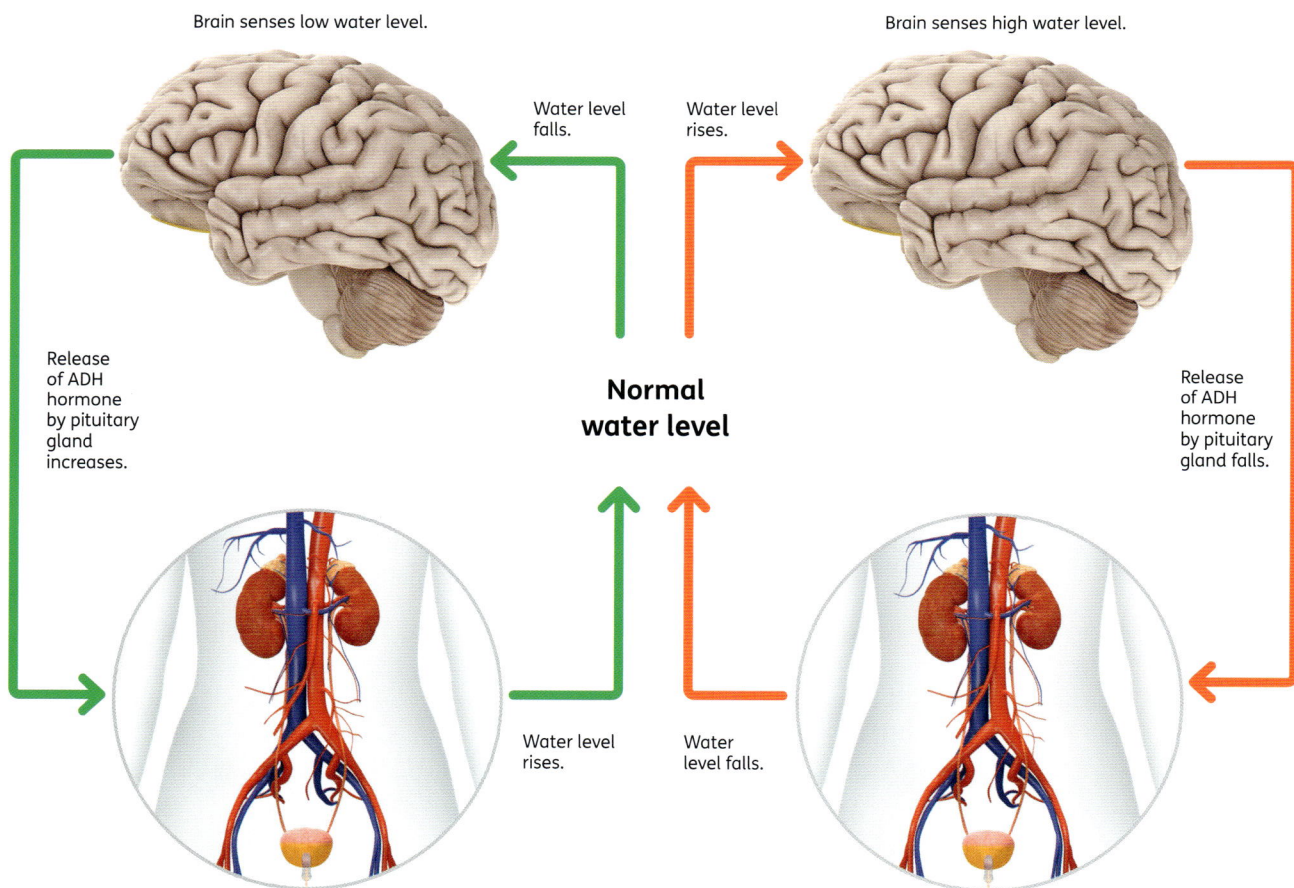

Brain senses low water level. — Water level falls. — Release of ADH hormone by pituitary gland increases. — Kidneys reabsorb water from urine. — Water level rises. — Normal water level

Brain senses high water level. — Water level rises. — Release of ADH hormone by pituitary gland falls. — Kidneys let more water into urine. — Water level falls. — Normal water level

Homeostasis and Response

Key facts

Urea is a waste product made by the liver as it breaks down excess amino acids.

Kidneys remove urea, as well as excess water and ions in urine.

Stages of urine production in a kidney:

- Filtration of blood (through the glomerulus and Bowman's capsule).
- Reabsoption of useful substance (for example, glucose, some ions, water if needed).
- Urine flows through ureters (tubes) into the bladder to be stored, ready for when you pass urine.

Filtration and reabsorption

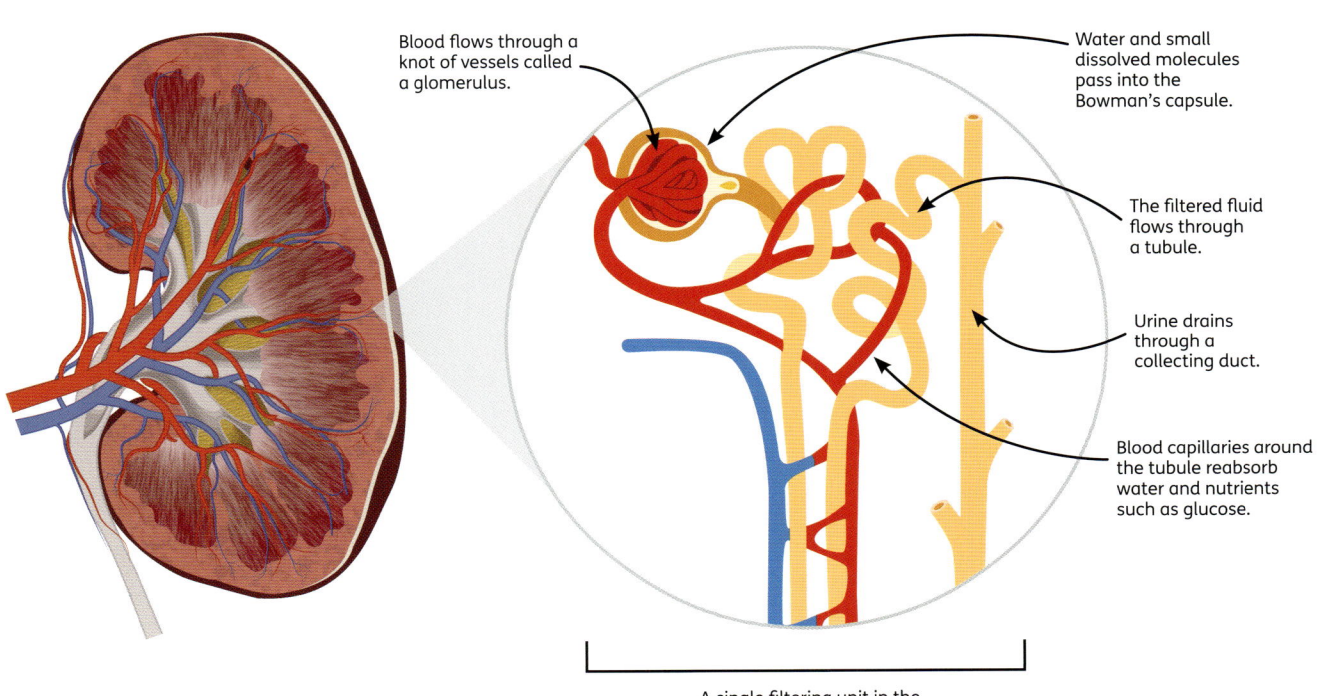

Blood flows through a knot of vessels called a glomerulus.

Water and small dissolved molecules pass into the Bowman's capsule.

The filtered fluid flows through a tubule.

Urine drains through a collecting duct.

Blood capillaries around the tubule reabsorb water and nutrients such as glucose.

A single filtering unit in the kidney is called a nephron.

Kidney failure can be treated using a transplant (replacing a kidney with a healthy donor kidney) or **dialysis**.

Blood is filtered through a machine. Waste substances, excess ions and water diffuse into the dialysis fluid. The fluid contains the same concentration of useful substances as blood, so glucose and some ions remain in the blood.

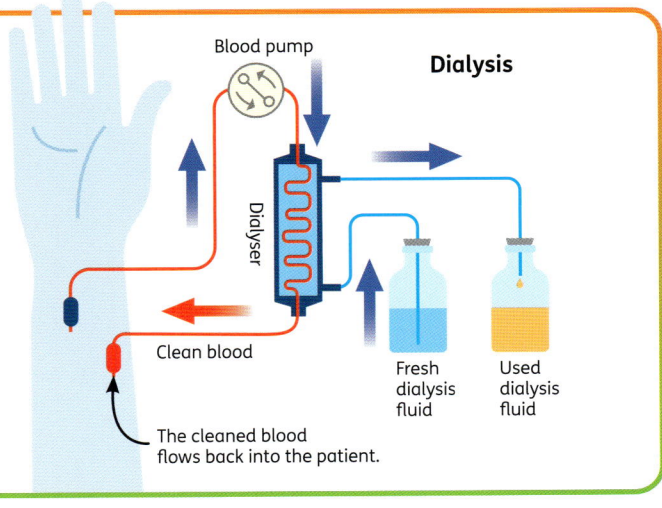

Reproductive Hormones

Key terms

- Follicle stimulating hormone (FSH)
- Luteinising hormone (LH)
- Menstrual cycle
- Menstruation
- Oestrogen
- Ovulation
- Progesterone
- Testosterone

Key facts

- During puberty, reproductive hormones are released:
    - Oestrogen from ovaries.
    - Testosterone from testes.
- They cause secondary sexual characteristics to develop.

Secondary sexual characteristics

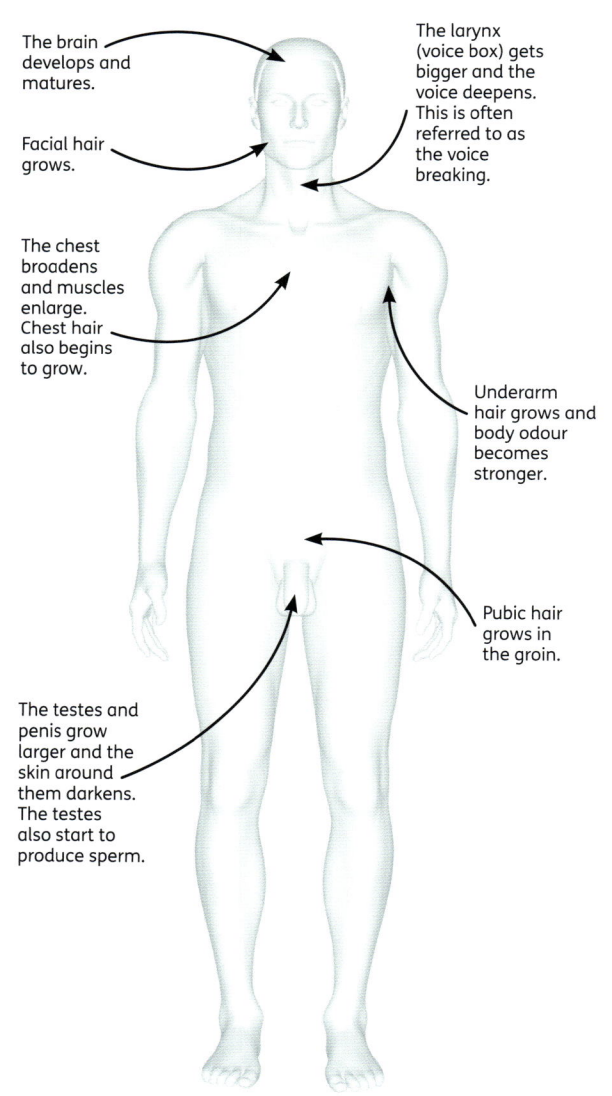

- The brain develops and matures.
- Facial hair grows.
- The larynx (voice box) gets bigger and the voice deepens. This is often referred to as the voice breaking.
- The chest broadens and muscles enlarge. Chest hair also begins to grow.
- Underarm hair grows and body odour becomes stronger.
- Pubic hair grows in the groin.
- The testes and penis grow larger and the skin around them darkens. The testes also start to produce sperm.

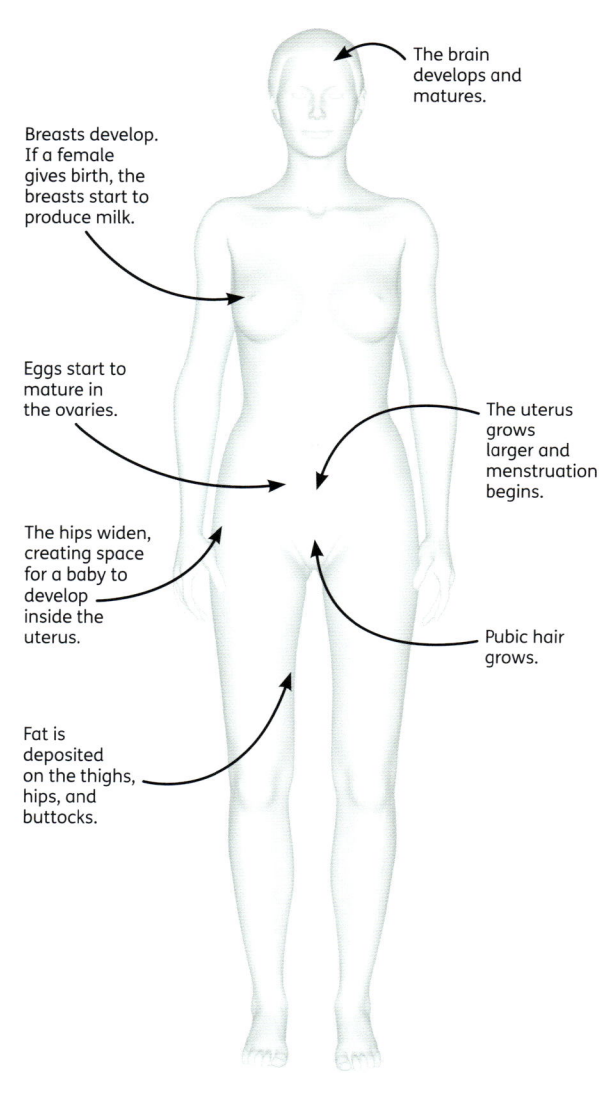

- The brain develops and matures.
- Breasts develop. If a female gives birth, the breasts start to produce milk.
- Eggs start to mature in the ovaries.
- The uterus grows larger and menstruation begins.
- The hips widen, creating space for a baby to develop inside the uterus.
- Pubic hair grows.
- Fat is deposited on the thighs, hips, and buttocks.

Homeostasis and Response

Menstrual cycle

The menstrual cycle begins in females during puberty and is controlled by hormones. Each month, the lining of the uterus is lost from the body through the vagina. The body then undergoes several changes to prepare it for a possible pregnancy. If pregnancy occurs, the cycle does not restart.

Approximate timing (days)	Event	Hormone trigger
1–5	**Menstruation** • uterus lining sheds with some blood.	Falling **progesterone**
	An egg cell in an ovary matures.	Rising **follicle stimulating hormone (FSH)**
6–14	Uterus lining thickens.	Rising oestrogen
14	**Ovulation** • release of mature egg cell.	Surge of **luteininising hormone (LH)**
15–28	Maintenance of uterus lining.	Rising **progesterone**

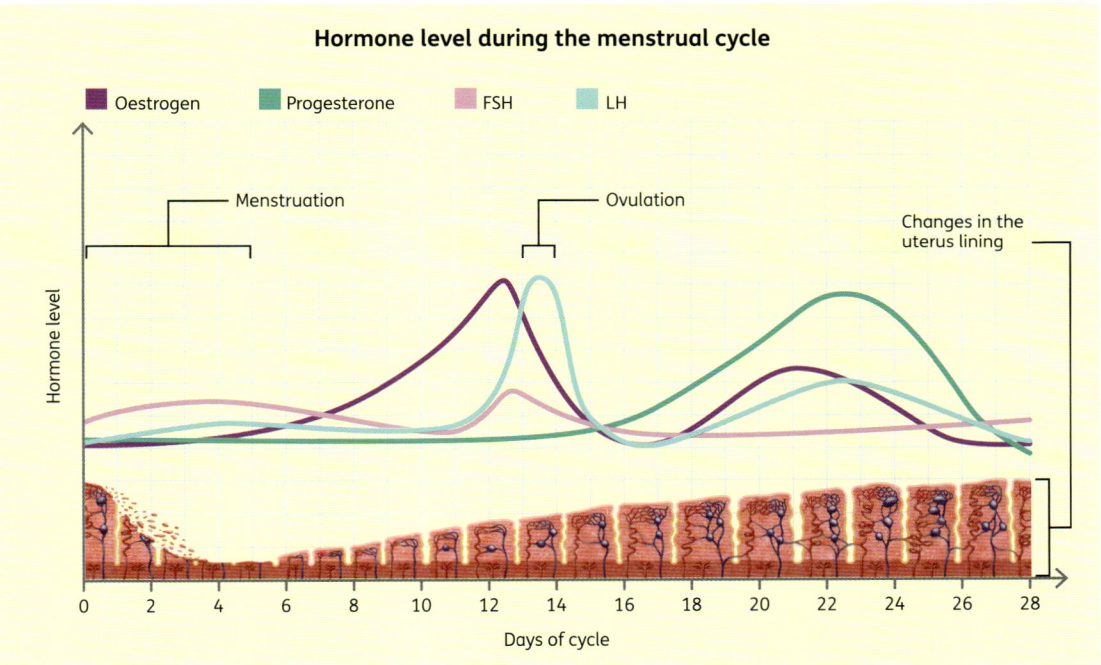

Science skills

Hormone levels are shown in the diagram as a line graph.

- Line graphs show changes of one variable with time. The points are usually joined dot-to-dot.
- Don't confuse line graphs with scatter graphs, which show a correlation between two variables using a line of best fit.

Blood hormone concentrations are tiny. For example, during the menstrual cycle, oestrogen concentrations rise to about 0.0000000008 g/cm³ of blood.

That is easier to read in standard form: 8.0×10^{-10} g/cm³

Or we can use an SI system prefix, to convert grams to nanograms: 0.8 ng/cm³

Homeostasis and Response

Contraception

Contraception is used to prevent pregnancy. There are hormonal and non-hormonal methods.

Key terms

- Abstinence
- Barrier method
- Contraception
- Ethics
- Intrauterine device (IUD)
- Sexually transmitted disease/infection (STD/STI)
- Sterilisation
- Spermicide

Hormonal methods

These use hormones that influence ovulation or egg maturation:

Type	Hormone	Action
Oral (pill) taken daily	Oestrogen and/or progesterone	Stops FSH production, so stops egg maturation.
Injection, implant or skin patch	Progesterone	Stops egg maturation and ovulation for months or years.
Hormonal intrauterine device (inserted into the uterus)	Progesterone	Thickens mucus in the cervix, which stops sperm cells entering.

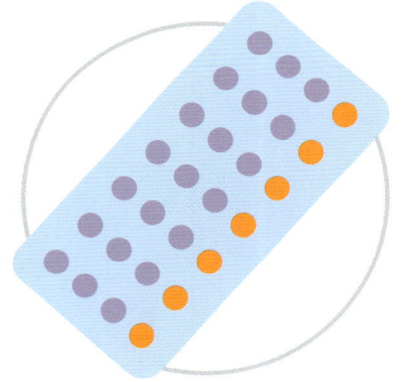

Oral contraceptives are tablets that may need to be taken every day.

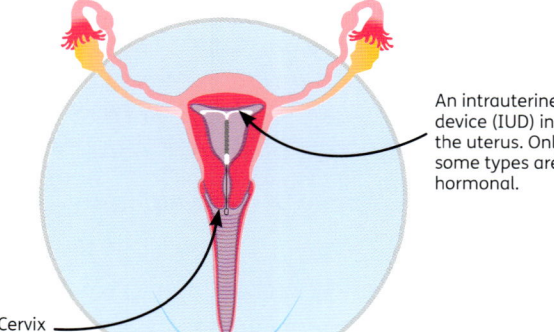

An intrauterine device (IUD) in the uterus. Only some types are hormonal.

Cervix

Science skills

Not all questions related to contraception can be answered by science.

Science can:
- Explain how contraception works.
- Provide evidence about effectiveness, side effects and health risks.
- Produce data to show the effects of contraception on populations and public health.

Science cannot:
- Answer questions based on religion, traditions or costs.
- Make decisions on what people think is right or wrong (**ethics**), such as contraception that stops embryo development by preventing implantation in the uterus.

Homeostasis and Response

Non-hormonal methods

Non-hormonal methods include:
- Male sterilisation surgery: prevents sperm cells being released from males.
- Female sterilisation surgery: prevents sperm cells reaching egg cells.
- Using barrier methods: prevents sperm cells reaching egg cells.
- Spermicide gel: kills or disables sperm cells.
- Intrauterine coil: contains copper to disable sperm cells and irritate the uterus lining to stop embryo implantation.
- Abstinence: not having sex, for example at times when an egg cell may be an oviduct.

Evaluation of contraceptive methods

Method	Advantages	Disadvantages
Hormonal	Highly effective, convenient	May have side effects (for example, mood changes). Need to remember to take pills.
Barrier	No hormones, protects against **sexually transmitted infections/diseases** (STIs/STDs)	Fail if used incorrectly.
Spermicide	Easy to use.	Not very effective on its own.
Sterilisation	Permanent	Needs surgery, irreversible.

Male condom

A condom fits over the penis. It collects semen and prevents sperm from entering the vagina. it also provides protection against sexually transmitted infections.

Female condom

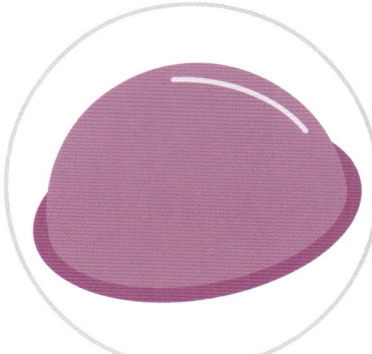

A diaphragm fits over the cervix. It is a thin rubber cap that is placed to prevent sperm to enter the uterus. It could be used with a spermicide cream that kills sperm.

Sterilisation

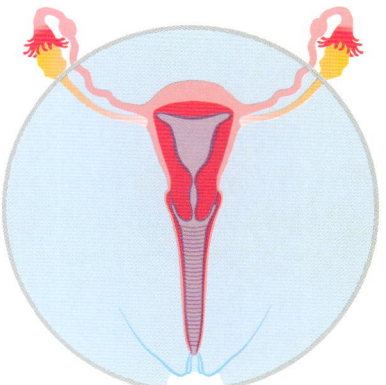

Male sterilisation involves an operation to prevent then having babies by cutting the tubes from the testes. Female sterilisation involves an operation to cut or clip the oviducts preventing eggs reaching the uterus.

Homeostasis and Response

Plant Hormones

Key terms

- Auxin
- Control variable
- Dependent variable
- Gravitropism (geotropism)
- Independent variable
- Phototropism
- Tropism
- Valid

Science skills

Investigating light direction on plant growth

- Put the same amount of cotton wool in two Petri dish bases.
- Add the same volume of water to each dish, to make the cotton wool damp.
- Add 10 cress seeds to each dish. Space them out evenly.
- Leave for a few days until shoots have grown from most of the seeds.
- Place one dish in a cardboard box with an open slot in the top.
- Place the other dish in a cardboard box that has an open slot in one side.
- Put the boxes in a warm place.
- Place lamps (of equal intensity and distance) pointing at the open sides of the boxes.
- After 7 days, make drawings and measure the lengths of the shoots. Calculate mean lengths.

In this experiment:

- Independent variable: light direction.
- Dependent variable: shoot length.
- Control variables for example, volume of water, number of seeds, temperature, length of time.

This is a valid method to measure the effect of light direction because only that one variable is changed. Something is valid if it does what it is supposed to do.

Results
The seedlings that grow sideways have slightly longer shoots.

Seedlings grow up towards the light.

Light from above

Seedlings grow sideways towards the light.

Light from one side

Homeostasis and Response 77

A **tropism** is a plant's response to a stimulus by growing in a certain way. It happens in slow-motion.

Phototropism and gravitropism are caused by a plant hormone called auxin. Unequal distribution of **auxin** causes unequal growth rates, and it has opposite effects in shoots and roots.

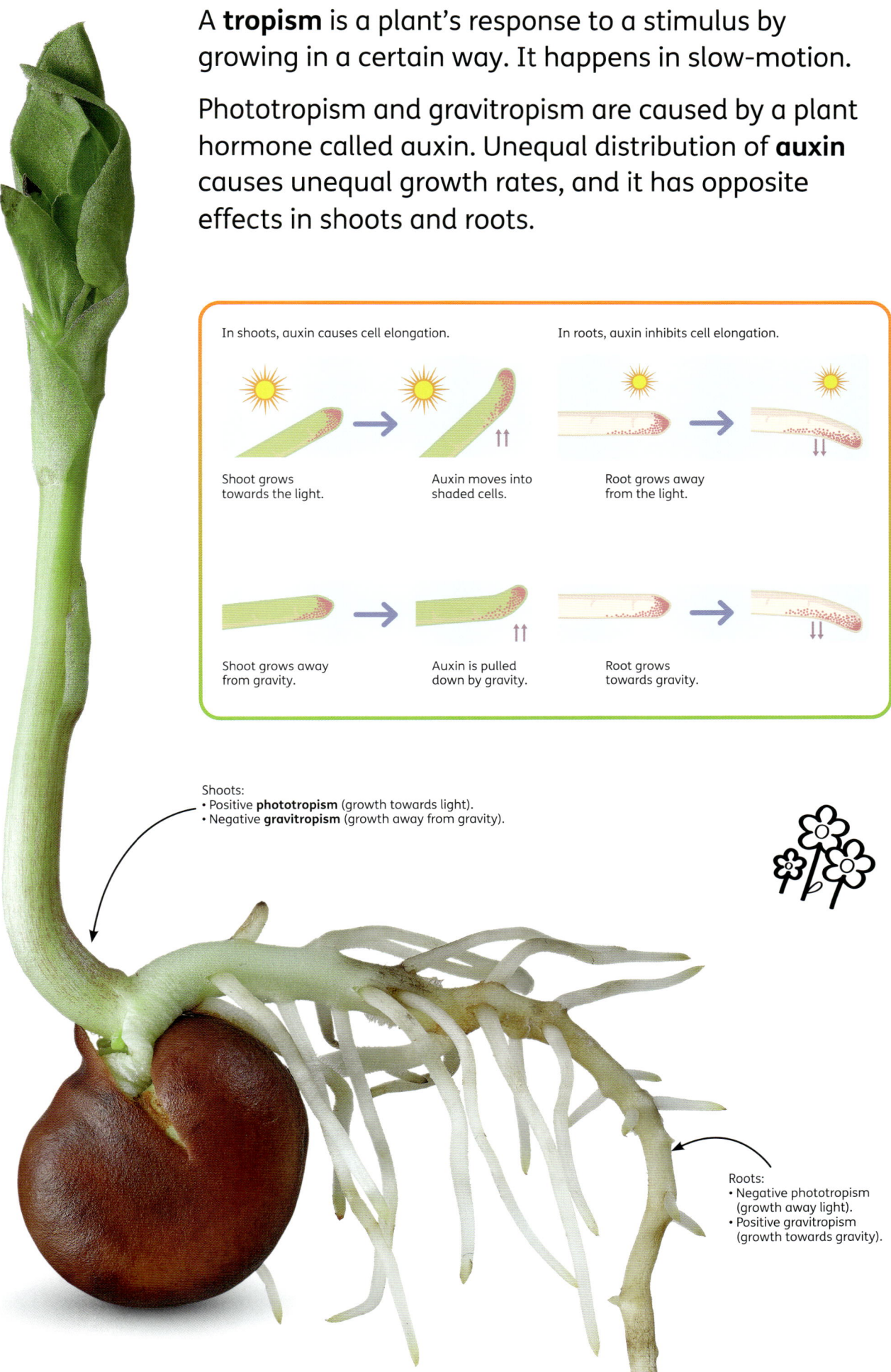

In shoots, auxin causes cell elongation.

Shoot grows towards the light.

Auxin moves into shaded cells.

In roots, auxin inhibits cell elongation.

Root grows away from the light.

Shoot grows away from gravity.

Auxin is pulled down by gravity.

Root grows towards gravity.

Shoots:
• Positive **phototropism** (growth towards light).
• Negative **gravitropism** (growth away from gravity).

Roots:
• Negative phototropism (growth away light).
• Positive gravitropism (growth towards gravity).

Brain Booster

Homeostasis and Response Recap Quiz

 Find a pen and paper and work through these revision questions.

1. Which organ is the main coordinator for temperature control in the body? Choose one.
   pancreas   liver   brain   kidney

2. What does the pancreas secrete to reduce blood glucose levels?
   insulin   adrenaline   oestrogen   glucagon

3. Give the name of the cells that carry electrical impulses to the CNS.

4. The flowchart shows how a stimulus causes a response. What are the missing words (a, b and c)?
   stimulus → **a)** → **b)** → **c)** → response

5. Give the name of the part of the eye in which you can find rods.

6. Give the name of the hormone that:
   a) causes ovulation   **b)** stimulates an egg cell to mature

7. **a)** State what is meant by "negative phototropism".
   b) Explain how the effect occurs.

8. Name **two** conditions in the body that are carefully controlled.

9. List the cells that can be found in a reflex arc.

10. How does the shape of the eye lens change when focusing on a distant object?

11. Outline **two** ways in which energy can be lost from the skin to the environment.

12. Give the name of the nitrogen-containing waste in urine.

Check your answers on page **109**.

Inheritance, Variation and Evolution

At the end of this chapter, you should be able to:

- ✓ Explain the advantages and disadvantages of sexual and asexual reproduction.
- ✓ Compare mitosis and meiosis.
- ✓ Explain how dominant and recessive alleles, and sex chromosomes have their effects.
- ✓ Use and interpret genetic cross diagrams, Punnett squares, family and evolutionary trees.
- ✓ Classify living things.
- ✓ Describe the role of DNA in making proteins.
- ✓ Explain why all populations have genetic variation.
- ✓ Explain evolution by natural selection
- ✓ Describe the roles of selective breeding and genetic engineering.

Inheritance, Variation and Evolution

Asexual and Sexual Reproduction

Reproduction is the process where organisms duplicate. Cell division is when a cell splits to form new cells.

Key terms

- Asexual reproduction
- Clone
- Meiosis
- Mitosis
- Sexual reproduction

Mitosis and asexual reproduction

Chromosomes store genetic information – the information that makes you "you". A body cell has two copies of each type of chromosome. Humans have 23 different chromosome types, so every human body cell has 46 chromosomes.

In **mitosis**, a cell duplicates all its chromosomes and then splits. Both **daughter cells** have two copies of everytype of chromosome. They are **clones** (see pages 94–95).

Asexual reproduction in yeast
Reproduction that makes identical copies of a parent is asexual. Yeast budding is an example.

The daughter cell is smaller than the mother cell.

A wall forms between the two cells before the daughter cell separates.

Meiosis and sexual reproduction

During **meiosis**, a cell splits and then splits again. The resulting four cells are **gametes**, and they are all genetically different. Animal gametes are sperm cells and egg cells. Plant gametes are pollen and egg cells.

Stages of meiosis
In **sexual reproduction**, two gametes fuse in a process called **fertilisation**. This forms a **zygote**. The mixing of different chromosomes from two different parents causes **variation** in the **offspring**.

1. Gamete-making cell duplicates each chromosome. The copies remain joined in the middle, forming X shapes.
2. Chromosomes of the same type swap sections of DNA with one another.
3. The cell divides.
4. Each cell divides again.
5. Each cell has just one set of chromosomes.

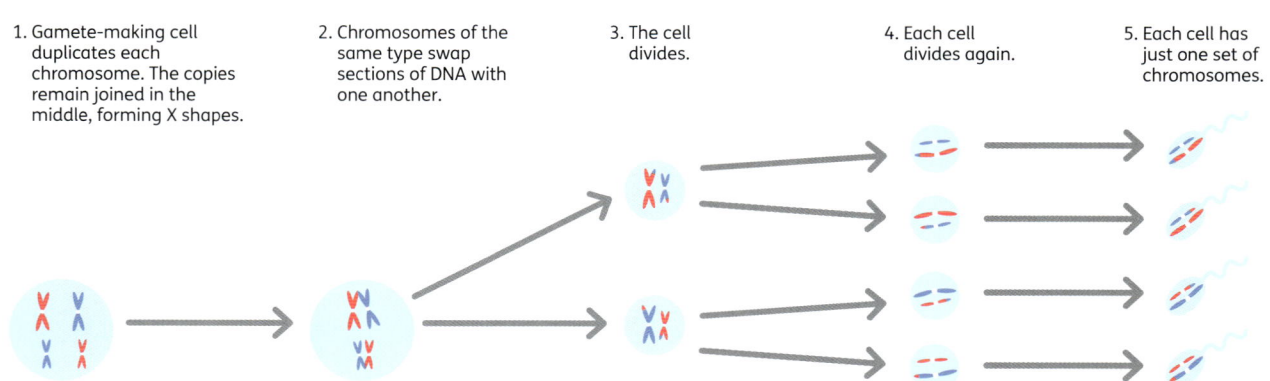

Inheritance, Variation and Evolution

Key facts

Sexual reproduction • Two parents • Variation	Produces variation. If there is an unfavourable change in conditions, some offspring may (by chance) have the right combination of genes to survive.	Produces fewer offspring. Slower because two parents are needed.
Asexual reproduction • One parent • No variation	The offspring are clones and so can survive in the same environmental conditions as the parent. Many offspring can be produced. Faster (there is no need to find a mate).	No variation. If there is an unfavourable change in environmental conditions, all the organisms may die.

How organisms reproduce

Most animals only reproduce sexually. Plants use sexual reproduction to produce seeds, but some reproduce asexually as well (for example, strawberry plants **runners**, daffodil **bulb division**).

Plasmodium reproduces sexually in mosquitoes. It gets into humans when mosquitoes suck our blood. Plasmodium reproduces asexually in humans and causes **malaria**.

Fungi also use both types of reproduction. For asexual reproduction, they use **spores**.

Runner

Runners are horizontal stems that grow along the ground and then take root, forming a new plant. Strawberry plants can reproduce this way.

Bulblet

Bulbs are underground food stores produced by many plants. They also produce new plants from "bulblets" around the base.

RAPPING UP!

School Biology – **reproduction**.
There are two types – I'll show you their functions.
The first one is, of course, sexual.
Gametes combine to make the set full.

How they combine – it's just meant to be.
Chromosome number? Each 23.
Those two sets, they both oughtta mix.
When they combine, it makes 46.

This process gives us variation,
or we'd be a clone **population**.
To make sperm and egg, here's the prognosis.
The process name, we call it **meiosis**.

Moving onto asexual.
The offspring come out identical.
There's only one parent – you need to know this.
The process here, we call it mitosis.

Each one has its own advantage.
Asexual is simply the fastest.
Sexual's slow, but that don't make it worse,
as the children come out way more diverse.

Inheritance, Variation and Evolution

DNA

Key terms

- Amino acid
- DNA
- Gene
- Genome
- Inherited disorder
- Nucleotide

Key facts

- Inside a cell's nucleus are **chromosomes**.
- Chromosomes contain a two-stranded **polymer**, twisted into a **double helix**. This is **DNA**.
- DNA is a type of **genetic material**.
- Genetic material contains coded instructions. This is called **genetic information**.
- Genetic information is found in stretches of DNA called **genes**.
- Genes each contain one code to make one specific **protein**.
- Proteins are formed of linked chains of different **amino acids**.
- Amino acids are joined in the order specified by a gene's **genetic code**.
- Genetic codes are shown using the letters A, T, C, and G.

DNA structure

DNA is a polymer made of repeating **nucleotide** units. Each nucleotide consists of:

- A sugar molecule (called ribose).
- A phosphate group (a group of phosphorus and oxygen atoms).
- A base from a choice of four types: A, T, C, or G.

There are four types of nucleotide, depending on which base it has. The order of the four bases creates a code for the order of amino acids in a protein.

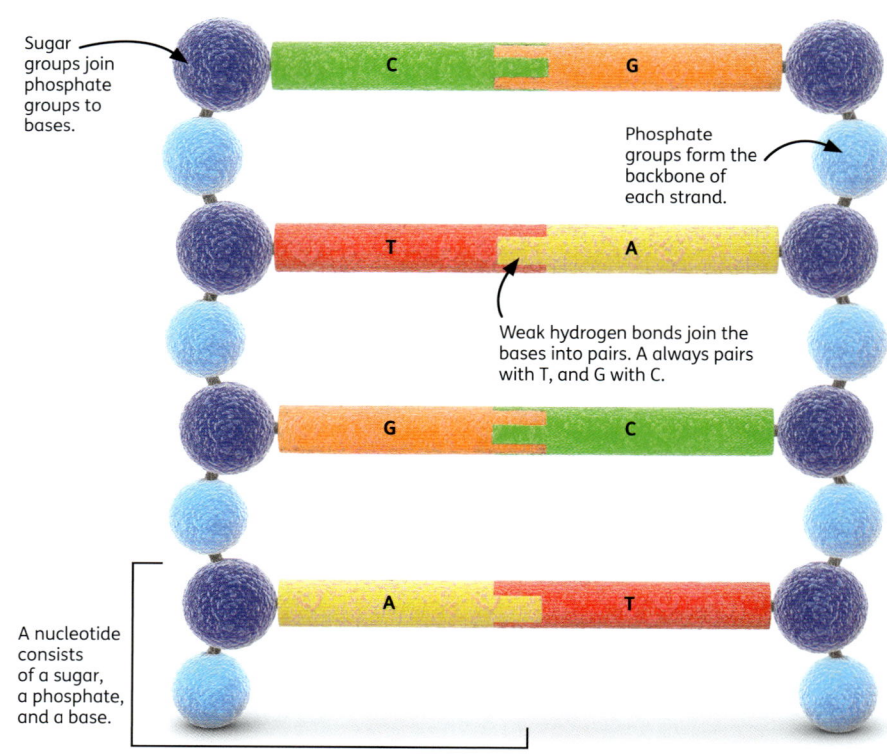

Sugar groups join phosphate groups to bases.

Phosphate groups form the backbone of each strand.

Weak hydrogen bonds join the bases into pairs. A always pairs with T, and G with C.

A nucleotide consists of a sugar, a phosphate, and a base.

Inheritance, Variation and Evolution

Genome

The **genome** is the entire genetic makeup of that organism. The **human genome** refers to the DNA that causes human characteristics, even though those characteristics vary between humans.

The Human Genome Project mapped out the human genome, which helps scientists:

- Find genes that cause certain diseases (**inherited disorders**).
- Develop treatments for inherited disorders, such as gene therapy to replace faulty genes.
- Find genes that may help to cause some other diseases.

Genomes change slowly over time. Scientists can use DNA analysis to track how organisms have spread over thousands of years – including humans spreading around the world.

Science skills

To extract DNA you can:

- Stir mashed fruit into a mixture of washing-up liquid, salt and water.
  - Detergent destroys membranes (the cell membrane and nucleus membrane).
  - Salt causes DNA molecules to clump together.
- Keep the tube at 60°C for 15 minutes.
- Filter.
- Add protease to filtrate. Protease breaks down proteins in the mixture.
- Very slowly add ice-cold ethanol. DNA is insoluble in ethanol and so forms a white precipitate layer.
- Use a glass rod to wind up the DNA and remove it from the tube.

RAPPING UP!

This right here? That's your **DNA**.
It's in every cell, every place, every day.
It's your blueprint, it has every trait.
It will tell us if your little or a heavyweight.

It's long I know, this gonna take practice:
deoxyribonucleic acid.
Say it a few times and make it rapid.
Two strands in a helix – the shape's drastic.

In the nucleus, it's a tiny **string**,
compressed into chromosomes like a spring.
Take a section – we call that a gene.
That section will code for a protein.

Between the two strands, what can you see?
Four bases: **A, T, C and G**.
The order of these bases, here you have it,
gives us the sequence of **amino acids**.

Genetic Inheritance

Key terms

- Allele
- Dominant
- Genotype
- Heterozygous
- Homozygous
- Phenotype
- Recessive

Traits

Most **traits** (characteristics of organisms) are controlled by many genes. However, some are controlled by just one gene. Examples include:

- Mouse fur colour.
- Red-green colour-blindness in humans.

So, how can mice have different fur colours and why aren't we all red-green colour-blind? It's because each gene has different forms, called **alleles**. Each allele has a slightly different genetic code.

Dominant and recessive

Body cells contain two copies of every type of chromosome, so they have two copies of every gene. These two copies of a gene may be the same allele or two different alleles.

The genotype of an organism is what alleles it has.

The phenotype is the effects of those alleles.

The fur colour gene in leopards has two alleles, D and d.

- The D allele gives a leopard its spots. It is dominant and so always affects the phenotype.
- The d allele gives black fur and is recessive. It only has an effect if both alleles are recessive.

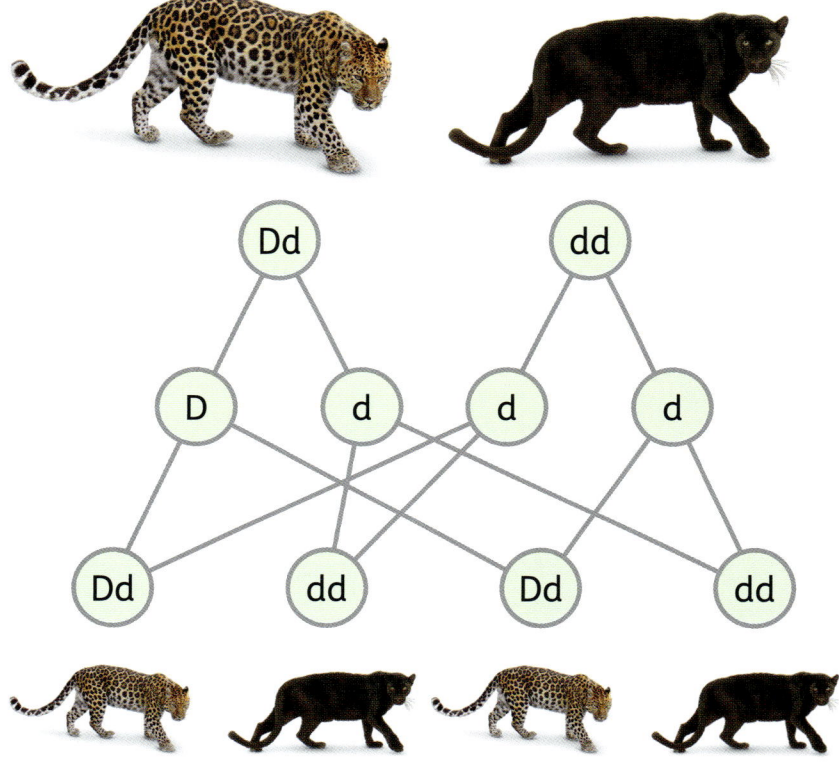

Genotype	DD	Dd	dd
Phenotype	spotted	spotted	black
Genotype description	homozygous (both alleles are the same) for the dominant fur allele	heterozygous (two different alleles)	homozygous for the recessive black fur allele

Inheritance, Variation and Evolution

Genetic cross diagrams

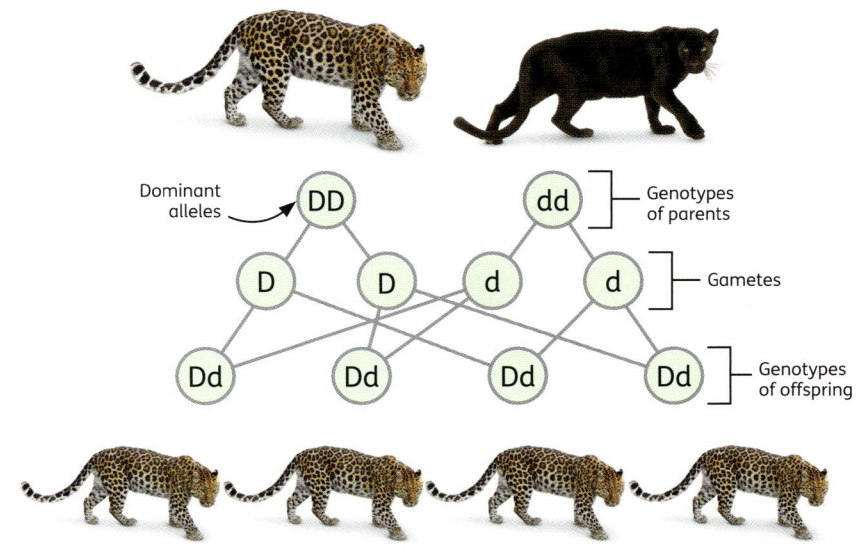

We can use **genetic cross diagrams** to work out the **probability** of phenotypes. If genotype DD mates with genotype dd, there is a 100 per cent probability that a cub will be spotted.

All the offspring have the same phenotype (spotted fur).

Punnett squares

We can also use Punnett squares. If two heterozygous leopards mate, this Punnett square shows a 3:1 ratio of spotty to black cubs. In other words, there is a 1 in 4 chance of a black cub (25 per cent).

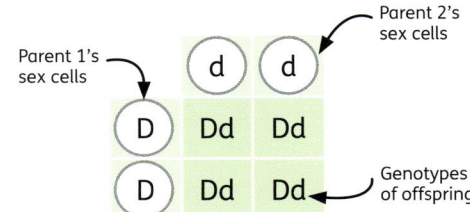

RAPPING UP!

Tim's **eyes** are blue but his folks' are hazel.
Is he adopted or was his mum unfaithful?
To answer this, I'll have to show you **Mendel**.
He cracked the code, I'll show you the essentials.

Mendel worked out **inheritance**.
He used pea plants as his evidence.
For every feature, you have two genes:
one from kings and one from queens.

Every gene has several types,
like all the colours if we look at eyes.
Listen close as I show the deal:
every gene type's called an **allele**.

A pair of these gives you features like
what you see – we call the **phenotype**.
In science terms, we know to write
the alleles in pairs – it's called the **genotype**.

Two of the same? It's called **homozygous**.
Learn that term – you ain't a so-so scientist.
One term left and I wanna let you try this.
Two different alleles we call that heterozygous.

For dominant traits you need one allele.
That's all you need in order to reveal.
For **recessive** traits you'll need two.
For hair it's blonde and for eyes it's blue.

Now back to Tim – let's put his mind at ease.
Both his parents have big and little Bs.
Tim took these so the **facts** are spoken.
He now knows his dad
is NOT the postman.

Inheritance, Variation and Evolution

Effects of Genes

> **Key terms**
> - Cystic fibrosis
> - Mendel
> - Polydactyly
> - Sex chromosome

Inherited disorders

Inherited disorders are caused by alleles and are passed from parents to their offspring.

- **Polydactyly**, caused by a dominant allele, results in extra fingers or toes.
- **Cystic fibrosis**, caused by a recessive allele, results in breathing and digestion problems due to faulty cell membranes.

A **family tree** can show a disorder's inheritance. A **carrier** has a recessive allele but not the disorder.

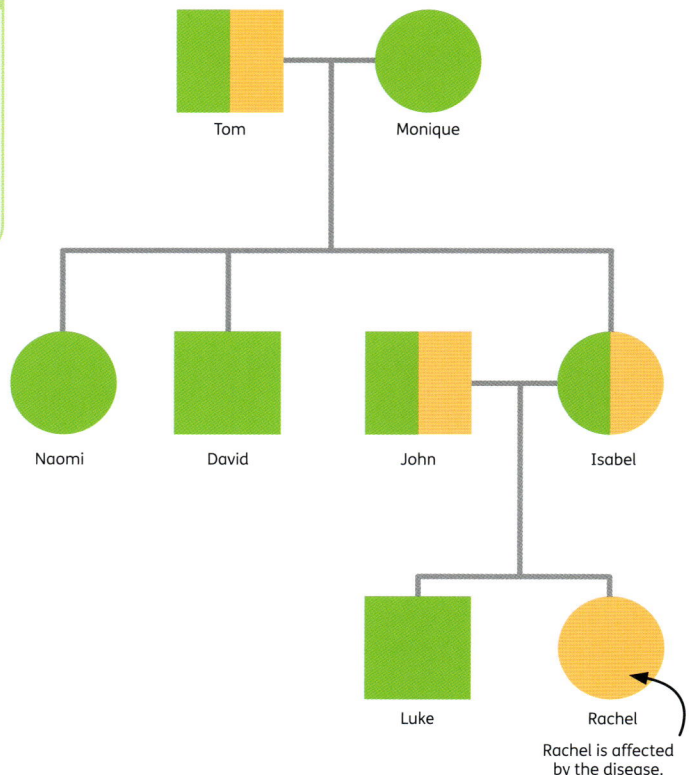

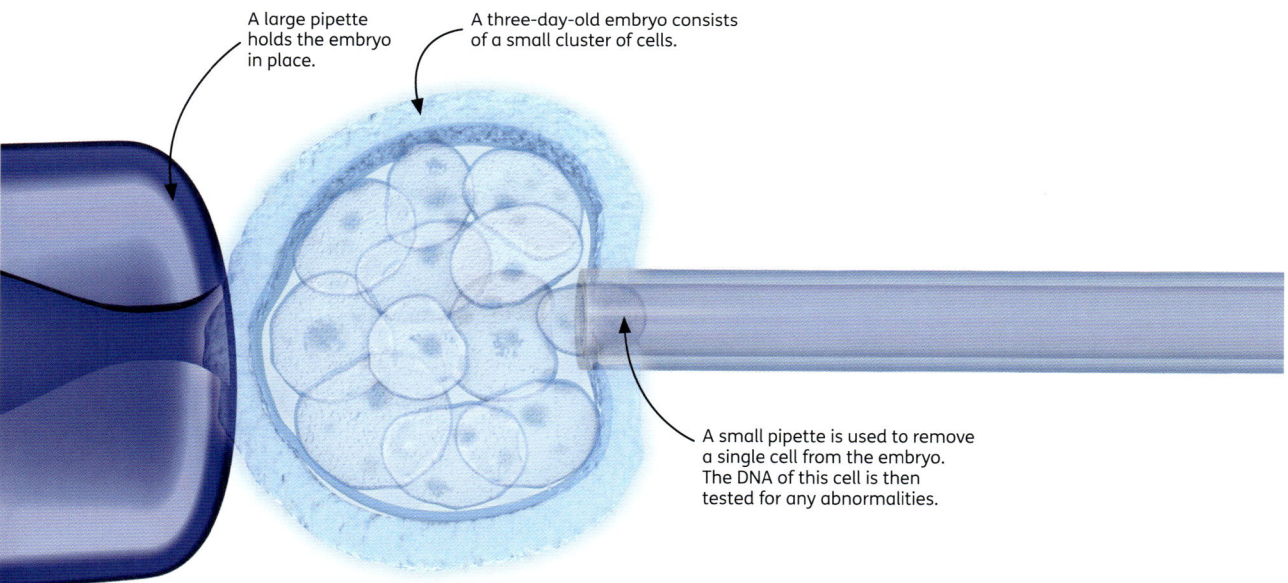

Embryo screening

Scientists can test embryos for inherited disorders when a woman is pregnant through **embryo screening**.

Inheritance, Variation and Evolution

Some people are against	Some people are in favour
Implies that people with inherited disorders are inferior.	Can stop suffering
Makes people want to have "designer" babies with certain characteristics.	Laws stop people selecting embryos with certain features.
Expensive for the health service.	

Sex chromosomes

Humans have 23 pairs of chromosomes. One pair, X and Y, are sex chromosomes and control sex. Females are genotype XX and males are XY. All female gametes have an X **sex chromosome**.

50 per cent of sperm cells have an X and 50 per cent have a Y.

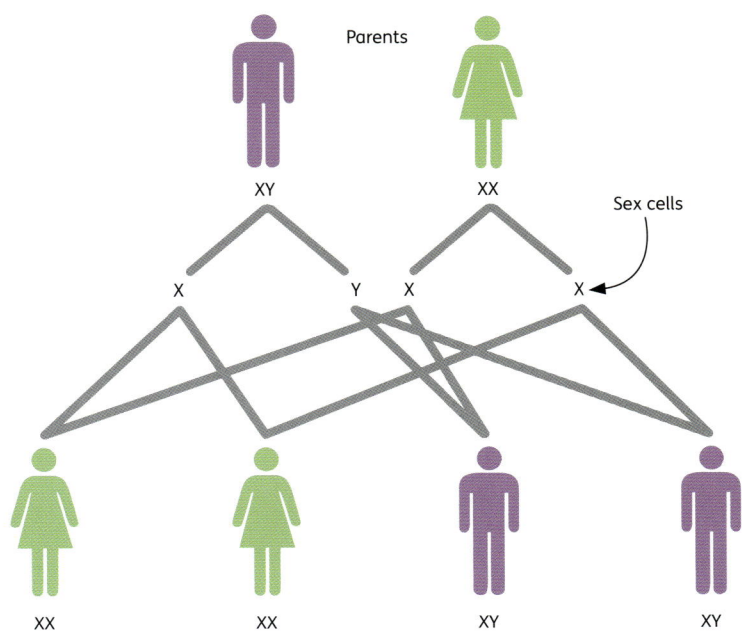

Blood group alleles

Your **blood group** (A, AB, B or O) is controlled by three alleles. IA and IB are **codominant** – they always produce their proteins. IO is recessive and does not produce a protein. You can only have Group O blood if you have two IO alleles.

Genotype	I^AI^A	I^AI^O	I^BI^B	I^BI^O	I^AI^B	I^OI^O
Phenotype	A	A	B	B	AB	O

Mendel

Gregor Mendel was an Austrian monk who bred pea plants in his monastery garden. He thought that "units" carried traits from one generation to the next. Some were dominant units, and others were recessive. We now call these "units" genes and alleles.

Mendel published his work in 1865. Scientists could not see how it worked and ignored it. But then:

- 1879: chromosomes were first seen to be involved in cell division.
- Early 20th century: chromosomes were shown to carry inherited traits in the same way as Mendel's units. Scientists concluded that Mendel's "units" were found on chromosomes.
- Mid-20th century: scientists discovered the structure of DNA and how genes make proteins.

Inheritance, Variation and Evolution

Variation and Classification

Key terms

- Archaea
- Bacteria
- Binomial system
- Domain
- Eukaryota
- Selective breeding

Key facts

Variation (differences) within a population of a species is caused by:

- Genetic factors – differences in alleles (for example natural hair colour).
- Environmental factors – conditions in an organism's surroundings (for example suntan, scars).
- Genes and the environment – (for example height is influenced by alleles and diet).

Genetic variation is due to genes having different alleles. A new allele is produced by mutations – random changes in the genetic code that occur all the time.

Most mutations have no effect; some have a small effect. Rarely does a mutation have a big impact. Sometimes, mutations cause variations that help an organism to survive. This can cause evolution (see page 90).

Selective breeding

Selective breeding (or "artificial selection") is when humans choose plants or animals with the best examples of a useful trait and breed them together. Doing this "selection and breeding" over and over again, produces new varieties of plants and new breeds of animals.

However, always selecting for the same useful traits in a population:

- Reduces the number of alleles (genetic diversity) – if not selected, they can disappear.
- Causes "inbreeding" – organisms become more likely to suffer from certain disorders.

Examples of selective breeding:

- Disease-resistant crops.
- Cows producing more milk.
- Livestock with more muscle for meat.
- Dogs with a gentle temperament.
- Bigger, more colourful flowers.

Farmers who kept choosing the fattest flower buds created cauliflowers and broccoli.

Breeding plants with a large, leafy main bud at the top created cabbages.

Choosing plants with large side buds created sprouts.

Breeding plants with the crinkliest leaves produced kale.

Choosing plants with the fattest stems produced kohlrabi.

Wild cabbage

Inheritance, Variation and Evolution

Types of classification

We still use Carl Linnaeus' system to group and name organisms by using their characteristics.

kingdom → animal (vertebrate)
↓ ↓
phylum chordate
↓ ↓
class mammal
↓ ↓
order primate
↓ ↓
family hominid
↓ ↓
genus *Homo*
↓ ↓
species *sapiens*

Binomial system: formula for a species name = genus + species (for example *Homo sapiens* for humans).

Recently, Carl Woese developed the three **domain** system using information from:

- Improved microscopes.
- Discoveries of chemical processes in cells.
- DNA analysis.

Domain	Organisms present
Archaea	Primitive bacteria in extreme environments
Bacteria	True bacteria
Eukaryota	Includes protists, fungi, plants and animals

RAPPING UP!

How can I be **homo sapiens**?
Let's talk about classification.
It's how you **categorise** living things
in seven groups and then you can name them.

Kingdom, phylum, class, order,
family, genus, then there's species.
Got the rhyme here that can support ya:
Kids Pick Candy Over Fresh Green Seaweed.

We're gonna focus on a **human being**
based on the characteristics you're seeing.
You place us in the animal kingdom
as we don't have cell walls on these things.

After kingdom we have **phylum**.
Got a backbone? Chordates our island.
For class we're all mammals,
the same as pandas and camels.

As for order, we're all **primates**,
and for family – Hominidae.
The last two lead to our naming,
So we call ourself homo sapiens.

Scientists use information from classification methods, DNA analysis and evidence from fossils to trace relationships between species and show how they have changed (evolved) over time.

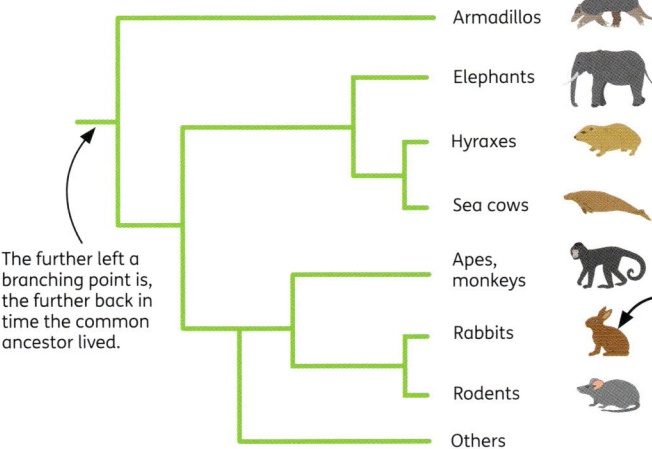

The further left a branching point is, the further back in time the common ancestor lived.

Although it may seem strange, these animals have similar DNA, which shows they have a common ancestor.

Rabbits share more DNA with rodents than with apes and monkeys.

Inheritance, Variation and Evolution

Evolution

Key terms

- Darwin
- Evolution
- Mutation
- Natural selection
- Species
- Wallace

Cause of evolution

Evolution is caused by mistakes when DNA is being copied. These mistakes or **mutations** happen continuously and change the sequence of As, Ts, Cs and Gs in a gene. Each allele has a different set of mutations.

Most mutations have little or no effect. Very rarely, a mutation changes an organism that may allow it to survive better than others. For example, to:

- Get more food.
- Cope with a change in environmental conditions.

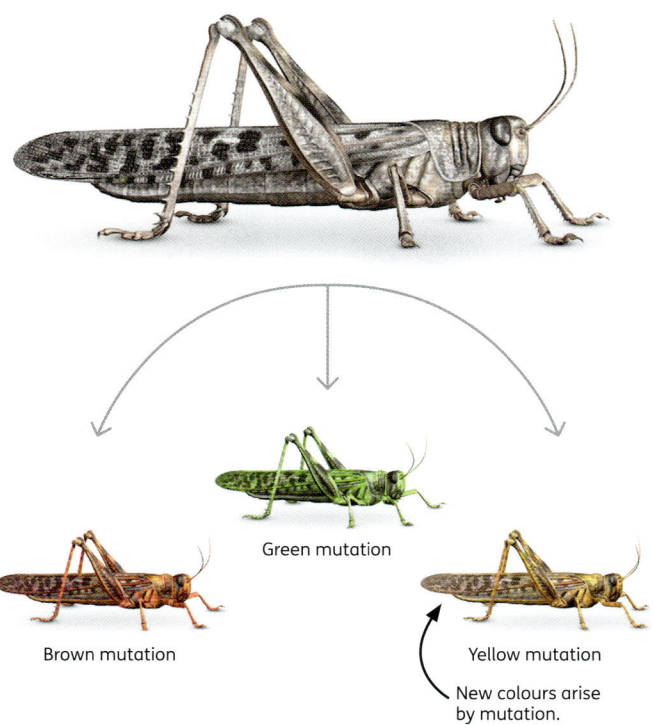

Brown mutation

Green mutation

Yellow mutation

New colours arise by mutation.

Natural selection

The longer the organism survives, the more likely it is to reproduce. If it reproduces, there is a chance that the beneficial mutation passes to its offspring, which then have more chance of survival. This is **natural selection**. Over time, more of the population display the advantageous characteristic.

Birds can see yellow and brown grasshoppers most easily.

Natural selection causes the population to change colour.

The green grasshoppers are well camouflaged.

Brown and yellow grasshoppers are well camouflaged.

Evolution of a new species

If natural selection continues in every generation, an entire population can slowly develop a new characteristic. This is evolution. With time, the changes can make the population into a new species that cannot breed with other populations.

A species is a set of similar individuals that breed to produce fertile offspring.

Important points:

- Natural selection happens to a population (not a whole species and not to individuals).
- Organisms do not choose to evolve. It is a game of chance.

Theories of Evolution

Key facts

- Today, scientists accept that all the Earth's species evolved from simple life forms, which developed over three billion years ago. But scientists were not always so sure.
- Charles Darwin and Alfred Russel Wallace both independently came up with this theory of evolution.
- The two scientists published their ideas together in 1858.
- Darwin then presented more of his evidence in 1859 in his book *On the Origin of Species*.

Theory acceptance

Darwin and Wallace's theory was not accepted by many people in the 19th century because:

- It did not include a divine creator.
- It could not explain how variation occurred.
- It could not explain how characteristics were inherited.
- Fossils seemed to show that evolution was not gradual – there were sudden jumps. (This was due to a lack of discovered fossils at the time.)
- There were other theories, for example, Jean-Baptiste Lamarck proposed that any changes to an organism in its life could be inherited by its offspring.

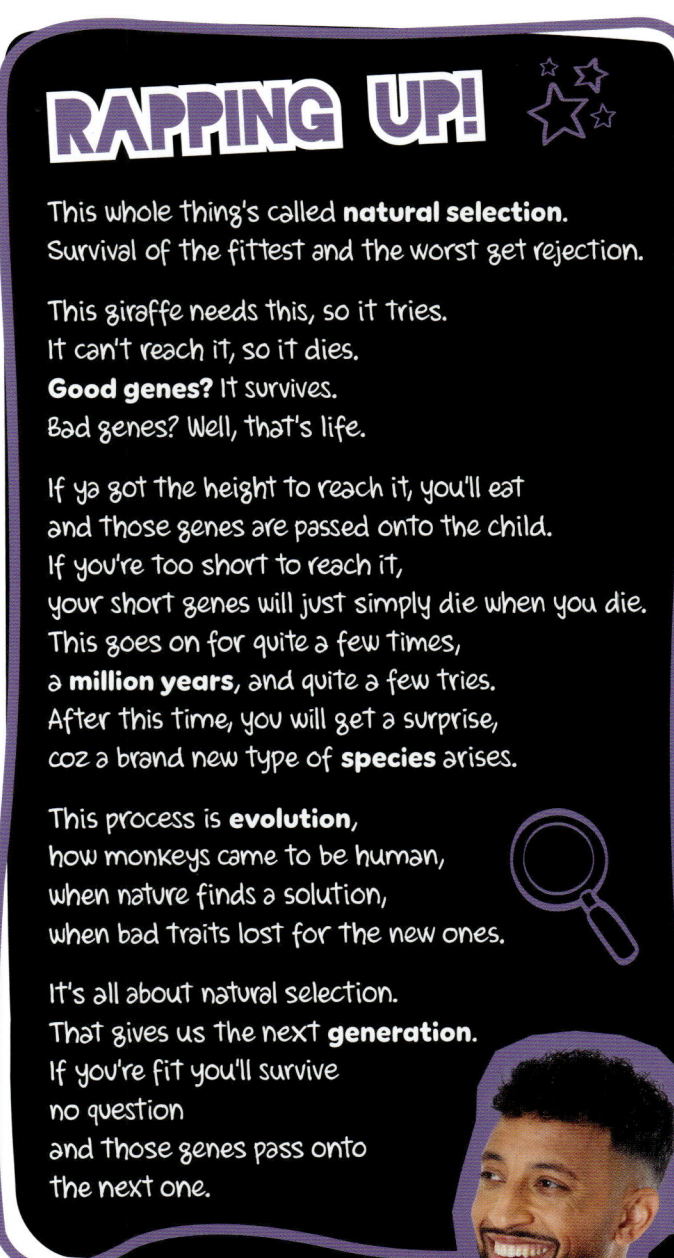

RAPPING UP!

This whole thing's called **natural selection**.
Survival of the fittest and the worst get rejection.

This giraffe needs this, so it tries.
It can't reach it, so it dies.
Good genes? It survives.
Bad genes? Well, that's life.

If ya got the height to reach it, you'll eat
and those genes are passed onto the child.
If you're too short to reach it,
your short genes will just simply die when you die.
This goes on for quite a few times,
a **million years**, and quite a few tries.
After this time, you will get a surprise,
coz a brand new type of **species** arises.

This process is **evolution**,
how monkeys came to be human,
when nature finds a solution,
when bad traits lost for the new ones.

It's all about natural selection.
That gives us the next **generation**.
If you're fit you'll survive
no question
and those genes pass onto
the next one.

Darwin collected much of his evidence for this theory of evolution on a voyage around the southern hemisphere in the 1830s. This included a lot of fossils.

Wallace was interested in the warning colours some animals had evolved to avoid being eaten. He travelled the world collecting this and other evidence for evolution by natural selection.

Inheritance, Variation and Evolution

Evidence for Evolution

Fossils

The fossil evidence for evolution by natural selection is much more complete today. Fossils can show how much or little organisms have changed over millions of years.

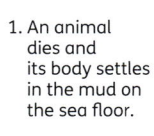

Key terms

- Fossils
- Extinct
- Antibiotic
- Antibiotic resistance
- Resistant

They may be:
- Preserved impressions such as footprints, animal burrows, holes made by plant roots.
- Undecayed parts of organisms – produced due to a lack of decay conditions (for example insects in amber).
- Rocky moulds – formed by minerals replacing rigid materials as they slowly decay (for example bones).

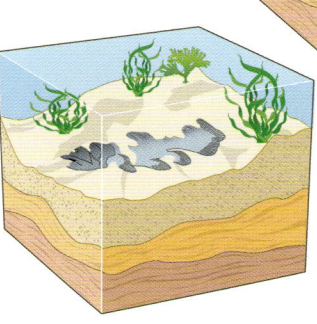
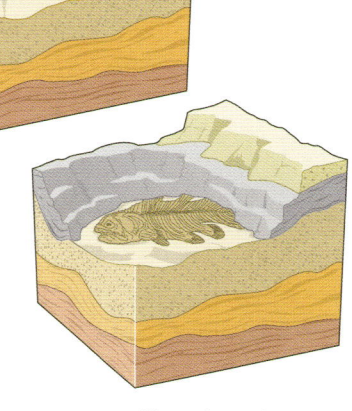

1. An animal dies and its body settles in the mud on the sea floor.
2. Sediment buries the body. Over time, the animal's remains and sediments turn to rock.
3. Millions of years later, movements in Earth's crust bring the fossil to the surface.

The soft parts of organisms decay quickly and do not often form fossils.

Fossil evidence is also destroyed by rock movements inside the Earth over millions of years. For these reasons, there are no fossils of the first organisms on Earth.

Dating fossils allows scientists to construct diagrams like this type of evolutionary tree. As more fossils are found, more information is added to the diagram.

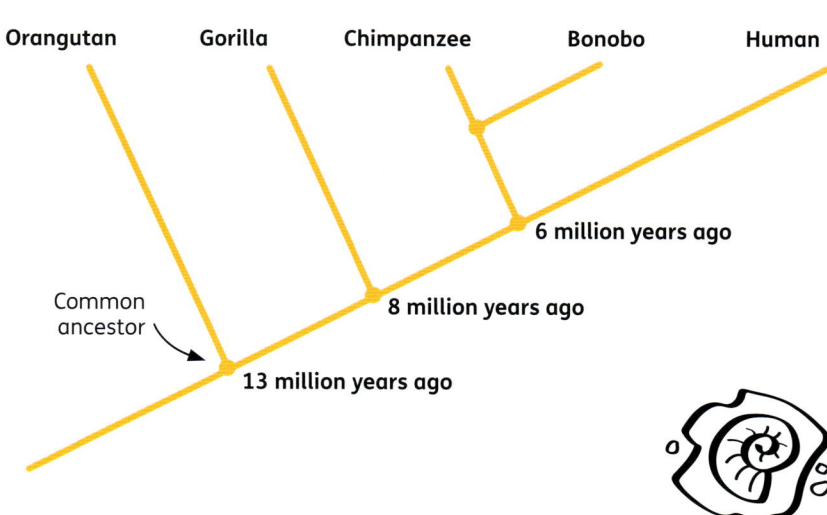

Inheritance, Variation and Evolution

Extinction

The common ancestors of most organisms are extinct. Extinction can be due to a:

- Sudden environmental change – such as the destruction of habitat.
- New predator that eats them all.
- Disease.
- New species arriving, which has better adaptations for getting food.

Human evolution

Collecting and examining hominid fossils has provided good information about human evolution. Over millions of years, the ancestors of humans got taller, walked more upright and developed larger skulls.

Million years ago	Names	Skull volume (cm^3)
0 (today)	Homo sapiens	1450
1	Homo erectus	850
2	Homo habilis	500–600
3	Lucy	400
4	Ardi	350

Scientists also study the development of hominid stone tools, going back 3.3 million years. Scientists can work out the age of a rock. When a tool is found in a rock, the rock's age gives the tool's age.

Antibiotic resistance

- More evidence for evolution by natural selection comes from antibiotic **resistance** in bacteria.
- The fast reproduction of bacteria means that they evolve quickly.

When resistant bacteria cause infections, fewer antibiotics can kill them. Developing new antibiotics is also expensive and slow.

To try to stop the evolution of antibiotic-resistant strains of bacteria:

- Doctors should not use antibiotics to treat non-serious or viral infections.
- Patients must take all their antibiotics so that all bacteria are killed and none can survive and mutate.
- Farmers should not give animals regular antibiotics to prevent sickness, only to treat sickness.

RAPPING UP!

This is **evolution**, here's the explanation.
It's when organisms change over **generations**.
This takes place over a million years,
at the end of this process a new species appears.

Caused by natural selection - I'll show you the steps.
Who gets to live and who dies is where nature selects.
I'm gonna give you an example, let's start with a human.
Let's go a million years back to see what we grew from.

Homo Erectus. I'm not being crude.
That's one of ancestors - the first of us to stand on two.
But there's a reason why they went into irrelevance.
A child was born with greater intelligence.

This child was better adapted and lived life like a King.
Which meant it lived longer and had more **offspring**.
If it had 10, then through inheritance
about three of the kids would have had the gene for intelligence.

If an **organism** is adapted well to where it lives
then it survives.
If it doesn't have the necessary adaptations then
believe that it dies.
That means good genes pass down, I bet that ain't a surprise.
This process carries on until a brand new species arise.

Inheritance, Variation and Evolution

Genetic Engineering and Cloning

Key terms

- Adult cell cloning
- Embryo transplants
- Genetic engineering
- Genetically modified organisms
- Tissue culture

Genetic engineering

Genetic engineering (or genetic modification) changes an organism's genes to make a **genetically modified organism (GMO)**.

It's done in a lab, often by taking genes from one organism and putting them into another. For example:

- GM crops – resist diseases and insect attack, resist certain **herbicides**, grow bigger, taste better.
- GM bacteria – produce useful substances, (for example human **insulin** to help people with diabetes).

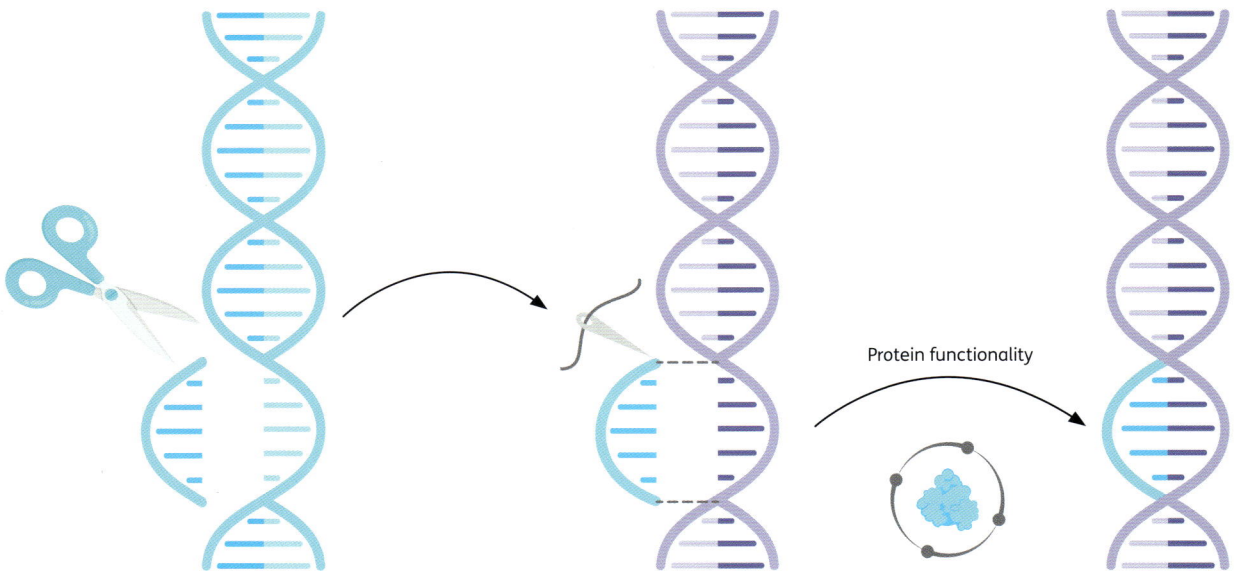

Benefits	Concerns
More growth for better yields.	We shouldn't interfere with nature.
Disease-resistant crops need fewer pesticides. (Many GM crops have genes for insect resistance from a bacterium, *Bacillus thuringiensis*.)	GM plants could escape from farms and harm ecosystems (especially insects and wildflowers).
GM technology can help cure some inherited disorders in humans.	GM food might have unknown effects.

Inheritance, Variation and Evolution

Key facts

- A **clone** is an identical copy.
- A simple traditional method of creating clones of plants is to take **cuttings**. A piece of a plant (for example a leaf) is planted and it grows into a new plant.
- Newer cloning methods can create more clones more quickly, including animals.

Tissue culture

In **tissue culture**, clumps of cells are treated to make them divide and grow. Great for:

- Making large quantities of the same plant for shops/farms.
- Increasing the numbers of rare plant species.
- Growing human cells for medical research, to avoid using animals.

Embryo transplants

Embryo transplants are used to create many clones from one embryo.

- Cells are taken from a developing animal embryo.
- In a growth solution, each one develops into another identical embryo.
- The embryos are transplanted into host mothers to grow, develop and be born.
- Multiple clones of farm animals with desirable characteristics are produced in this way.

In **adult cell cloning** the nucleus of a cell from an adult animal is used to produce a clone.

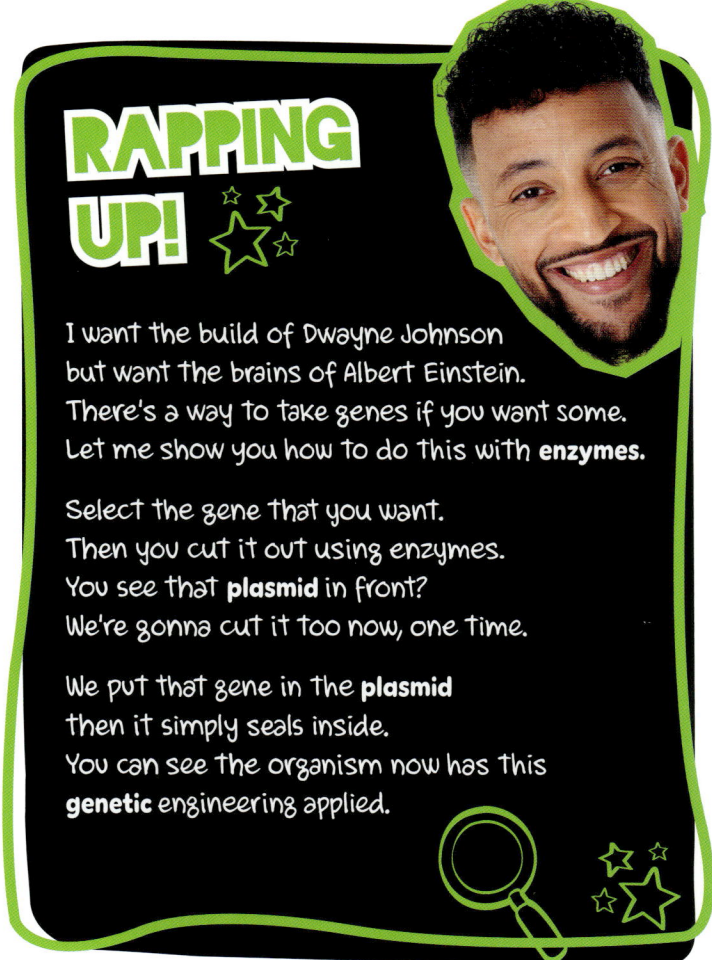

RAPPING UP!

I want the build of Dwayne Johnson but want the brains of Albert Einstein.
There's a way to take genes if you want some.
Let me show you how to do this with **enzymes**.

Select the gene that you want.
Then you cut it out using enzymes.
You see that **plasmid** in front?
We're gonna cut it too now, one time.

We put that gene in the **plasmid** then it simply seals inside.
You can see the organism now has this **genetic** engineering applied.

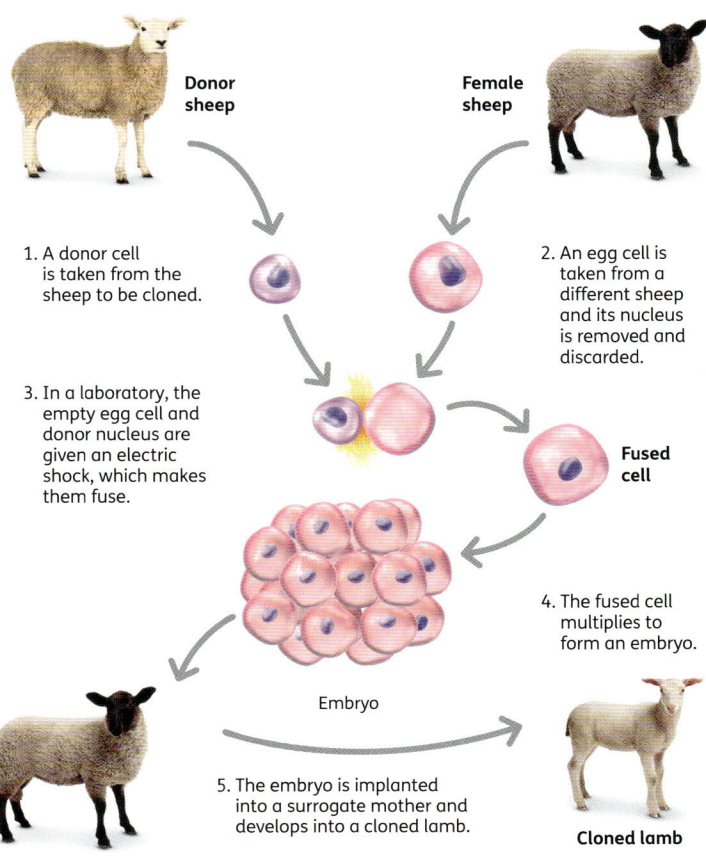

Donor sheep | Female sheep

1. A donor cell is taken from the sheep to be cloned.
2. An egg cell is taken from a different sheep and its nucleus is removed and discarded.
3. In a laboratory, the empty egg cell and donor nucleus are given an electric shock, which makes them fuse.
4. The fused cell multiplies to form an embryo.
5. The embryo is implanted into a surrogate mother and develops into a cloned lamb.

Fused cell

Embryo

Cloned lamb

Brain Booster

Inheritance, Variation and Evolution Recap Quiz

 Find a pen and paper and work through these revision questions.

1. Which type of reproduction creates clones? Choose one.
   sexual   asexual   neither   both

2. Which of these organisms reproduce both sexually and asexually? Select all that apply.
   strawberry   human   daffodil   cat   parrot   elephant

3. After fertilisation, name the process that occurs to produce an embryo.

4. Name the process that halves the number of chromosomes in a gamete.

5. State the components in a DNA nucleotide.

6. Give one reason why people are against embryo screening.

7. Give the name of an inherited disorder in humans caused by a dominant allele.

8. Give a reason why the theory of evolution was not accepted by everyone when it was proposed.

9. Give the reason why a fossilised skeleton in a museum contains no real bones.

10. Explain one reason why crop plants are genetically engineered.

Check your answers on page **109**.

Ecology

At the end of this chapter, you should be able to:

- ✓ Describe how ecosystems are organised.
- ✓ Explain how organisms both compete with and depend on one another.
- ✓ Identify and explain the effects of biotic and abiotic factors.
- ✓ Describe how some organisms have adaptations to help them survive.
- ✓ Construct and interpret food chains and pyramids of biomass.
- ✓ Describe how energy flows through ecosystems.
- ✓ Describe how materials are recycled in nature.
- ✓ Explain the effects of humans on biodiversity.
- ✓ Explain some ways in which we can live more sustainably.

Ecology

Communities

Key terms

- Abiotic factor
- Adaptation
- Biotic factor
- Community
- Competition

Ecology

Ecology studies the effects of living things and their environments on one another.

- **An individual** – one single organism.
- **Habitat** – the name of a place where an organism usually lives.
- **Population** – number of individuals of the same species living in an area.
- **Community** – names of all the different species in an area.
- **Ecosystem** – all the living things and the environmental conditions in an area.

An ecosystem is like a giant jigsaw. The environmental conditions and all the different organisms affect one another to form the whole picture. To survive and reproduce, all the species in an ecosystem depend on others in some way – for food, shelter, pollination, seed dispersal. This is interdependence.

In a stable community, the biotic and abiotic factors are balanced, and so populations remain steady. If a species disappears or a new one arrives, the ecosystem becomes unbalanced and populations change.

A grassland ecosystem in Africa

A community consists of all the organisms that interact in an ecosystem.

A habitat is a place where an organism is usually found. For example, termites build large nests in the ground.

All the organisms of a particular species in a specific area make up a population.

Organisms have adaptations to their habitat that help them survive. For example, this giraffe can feed on the leaves high up on tall trees with the help of its long neck.

Ecology

Biotic factors
Biotic factors are the living factors that affect an ecosystem.

- **Disease** – new pathogens can wipe out many individuals, or even a whole species.
- **Food availability** – organisms will die if they don't get enough food.
- **Predators** – more predators can mean fewer prey.
- **Competition** between species:
  - Animals compete for food, water, space, mates.
  - Plants compete for light, air, water, nutrients (mineral ions).

Abiotic factors
Abiotic factors are the non-living factors that affect an ecosystem.

- **Light intensity** – more light → more photosynthesis → plants have more food.
- **Temperature** – metabolism and survival rates change if it is too hot or too cold.
- **Water levels** – too little or too much → organisms die.
- **Soil pH** – different plants grow better in different pHs.
- **Minerals** – plants get mineral ions from soil, animals get mineral ions from food.
- **Wind strength** and direction – winds dry plants out, knock them over or change their shapes.
- **CO_2 levels** – plants need CO_2 for photosynthesis.
- **O_2 levels** – crucial in water for fish and other aquatic life.

Adaptations in desert plants

Photosynthesis takes place in the green surface layers of the stem.

The fleshy stem stores water.

The thick, waxy cuticle reduces the amount of water loss.

Instead of leaves, cacti have spines. This reduces the surface area and in turn restricts the amount of water lost through evaporation.

Stomata lie in pits on the surface of the stem, and only open at night so that less water evaporates.

Shallow roots spread out to absorb as much water as possible when it occasionally rains.

Adaptations
Each species has its own built-in mechanisms to survive. We call these adaptations.

- Behavioural adaptions – organism actions, for example **nocturnal** animals avoid heat or predators.
- Functional adaptations – internal processes, for example **deciduous** trees lose leaves to save water and energy.
- Structural adaptations – physical features, for example a polar bear's wide feet stop it sinking into the snow.

Extremophiles are organisms that can survive very high temperatures, pressures or salt concentrations. Some bacteria survive in deep sea thermal vents, where temperatures can be 80–110°C.

Ecosystem Organisation and Energy Transfer

Key terms

- Abundance
- Biomass
- Consumer
- Decomposer
- Efficiency
- Estimate
- Mean
- Producer
- Pyramid of biomass
- Quadrat
- Sample
- Trophic level

Science skills

The mean is one of three types of average.
- **Mean** – add all the values together and divide by the number of values.
- **Mode** – the most common value.
- **Median** – the middle value when arranged in order.

Food chains
The arrows → in a food chain show energy flow.

Nettle → Caterpillar (of tortoiseshell butterfly) → Cuckoo (small bird) → Sparrowhawk (large bird)

Trophic level 1	Trophic level 2	Trophic level 3	Trophic level 4
Producer – usually plants or **algae** that use **photosynthesis** to make glucose	**Primary consumer** – all consumers need to eat	Secondary consumer	Tertiary consumer
	Herbivore (eats plants)	**Carnivore** (eats animals)	Carnivore
		Predator of caterpillars **Prey** of sparrowhawks	**Apex** or **top predator** (a predator that is not prey)

As well as producers and consumers, there are decomposers. These bacteria and fungi secrete enzymes to digest plant and animal waste. This process releases nutrients and mineral ions, which are absorbed by the decomposers and reused.

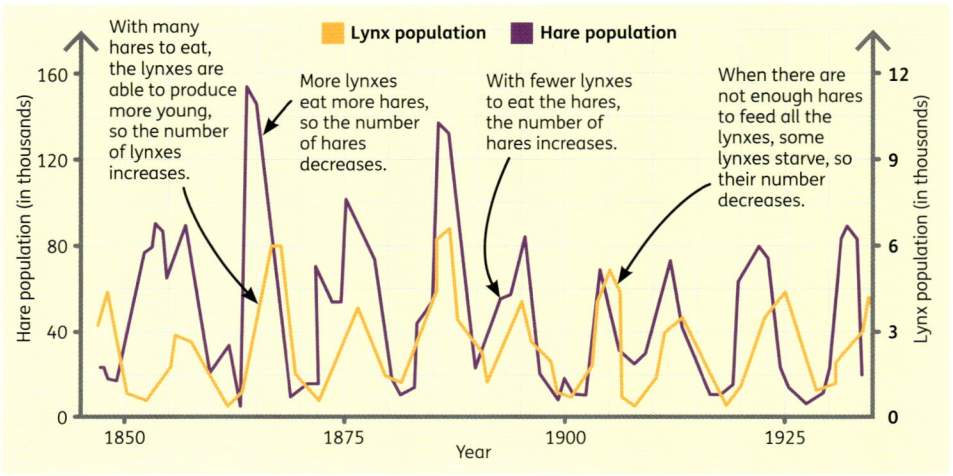

Predator–prey relationships
In a stable community, the numbers of predators and prey rise and fall in cycles (more predators mean fewer prey, and vice versa). For example, lynxes are predators of snowshoe hares in the Arctic.

Ecology

Sampling

Abundance is a measure of how common an organism is. For common organisms, it's very difficult and time-consuming to count all the individuals. Therefore scientists take **samples** and calculate an **estimate**.

For small plants and very slow animals, we take samples using a **quadrat**.

- The quadrat is placed randomly in an area. This stops results being influenced by the scientist.
- The number of organisms inside the quadrat is counted.
- The process is repeated many times.

Pyramids of biomass

Pyramids of biomass show the mass of living things at each trophic level. Level 1 (producers) are at the bottom.

A pyramid shape forms because the mass of organisms ("biomass") is less at each level.

- Not all the food a consumer **ingests** is digested – some is **egested**.
- Glucose is used up in respiration.
- Materials are lost in wastes, such as carbon dioxide and urea.
- Some organisms in a trophic level are just lucky – and don't become dinner.

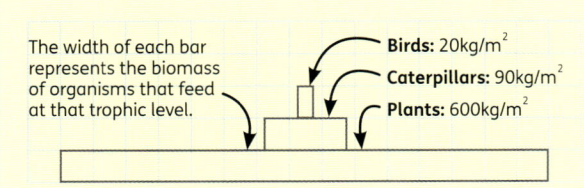

Birds: 20kg/m^2
Caterpillars: 90kg/m^2
Plants: 600kg/m^2

The width of each bar represents the biomass of organisms that feed at that trophic level.

Energy transfer

About 1 per cent of the energy transferred by sunlight is transferred into the substances made by producers. About 10 per cent of the energy in a trophic level is transferred to the next level.

Less energy in a level = fewer organisms. That is why food chains rarely contain more than four organisms – there's no more energy.

Science skills

1. Work out the mean number of the organism per m^2.

   Mean number of organisms = $\dfrac{\text{Total number of organisms counted}}{\text{Total area in m}^2 \text{ of all the quadrat samples}}$

2. Total population estimate = Mean number of the organism per m^2 × Total area of habitat in m^2

Using a quadrat

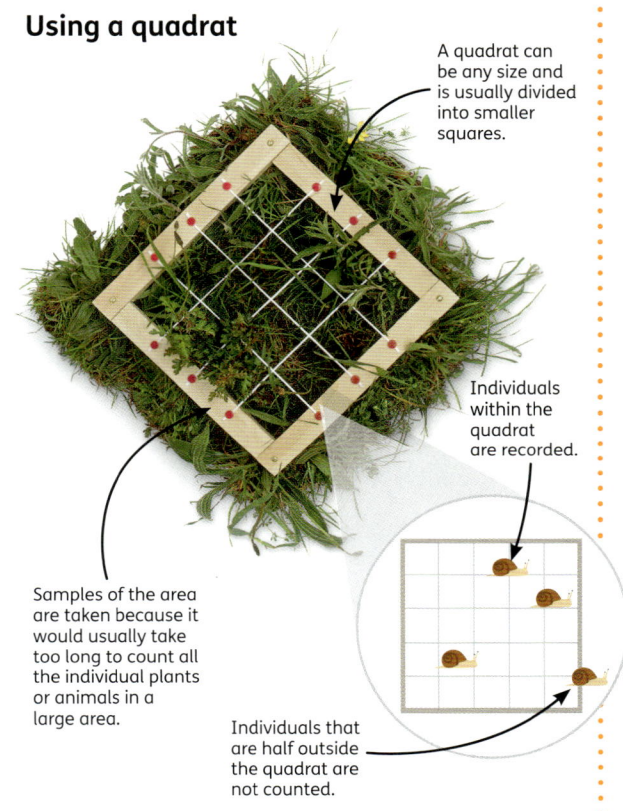

A quadrat can be any size and is usually divided into smaller squares.

Individuals within the quadrat are recorded.

Samples of the area are taken because it would usually take too long to count all the individual plants or animals in a large area.

Individuals that are half outside the quadrat are not counted.

Science skills

Calculate the **efficiency** of transfers between trophic levels (biomass or energy).

Efficiency(%) = $\dfrac{\text{Biomass in trophic level above}}{\text{Biomass in trophic level beneath}}$

Ecology

Natural Cycles

Key terms

- Aerobic respiration
- Anaerobic respiration
- Biogas generator
- Carbon cycle
- Compost
- Manure
- Nitrates
- Nitrogen cycle
- Nitrogen-fixing
- Rate
- Water cycle

Rate of decomposition

The **rate** (speed) of decomposition depends on:

- Temperature: warm conditions (30–60°C) speed up decay because enzymes work faster. However, too hot, and enzymes stop working because they become denatured.
- Oxygen: more oxygen allows more **aerobic respiration** and faster decay. Too little oxygen causes **anaerobic respiration**, which makes methane and slows decay.
- Water: all reactions in cells occur in liquids. If decomposers dry out, they die. However, too much water slows the supply of air (with O_2) and causes anaerobic conditions.

Cold temperatures, removal of oxygen and drying are used to stop food decomposing.

Sometimes anaerobic respiration is useful. **Biogas generators** turn organic waste into fuel using anaerobic decomposition. The methane is burnt for energy. This is **renewable** and removes waste.

Decomposition

An ecosystem's **decomposers** (fungi and bacteria) feed on animal waste and dead organisms. This:

- Removes dead organisms.
- Removes animal waste.
- Releases mineral ions back into the soil, which other organisms use again.

Gardeners turn kitchen scraps into **compost**. Farmers mix animal faeces and straw to make **manure**. Both use decomposers to form natural fertilisers for plants.

Science skills

Materials become more acidic (the pH gets lower) during decomposition.

You can calculate the rate of decomposition by measuring a decrease in pH or mass over time.

Rate of decay =

$$\frac{\text{Mass or pH at start} - \text{Mass or pH at end}}{\text{Time}}$$

For example:

- Make an alkaline solution of milk at pH 8.8.
- Add lipase (an enzyme that breaks down fats into fatty acids).
- Add cresol red (an indicator that is purple in alkaline solutions but yellow below pH 7.2).
- Divide identical volumes of milk into tubes at different temperatures.
- The less time for a tube to go yellow (or not purple), the faster the rate of decomposition.

Cycling water

The water cycle provides fresh water for plants and animals on land before draining into the seas.

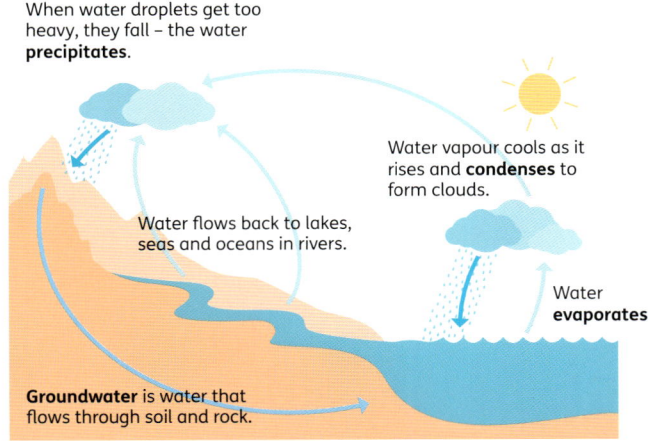

When water droplets get too heavy, they fall – the water **precipitates**.

Water vapour cools as it rises and **condenses** to form clouds.

Water flows back to lakes, seas and oceans in rivers.

Water **evaporates**

Groundwater is water that flows through soil and rock.

Cycling nitrogen

The **nitrogen cycle** shows the processes that cycle nitrogen through the soil, food chains and the air.

- Plants need **nitrates** to make proteins.
- **Nitrogen-fixing** – a process in which nitrogen from the air is converted into compounds.

Cycling carbon

The **carbon cycle** shows the processes that cycle carbon through the soil, food chains and the air.

- Respiration
- Combustion/Carbonate breakdown
- Death/Decomposition
- Photosynthesis
- Rock formation

Carbon dioxide is given out by plants as a waste product of respiration.

All animals release carbon dioxide into the air during respiration.

Animals take in carbon compounds when they eat food.

Combustion (burning) of fossil fuels and wood releases carbon dioxide into the atmosphere.

Plants and algae convert carbon dioxide to sugars during photosynthesis.

Animal faeces and urine

Animals die

Processes such as weathering release carbon dioxide from carbonates in rocks.

Bacteria, fungi, and soil animals break down dead and waste matter, releasing carbon dioxide during respiration.

Dead matter forms sediments, which are compacted over millions of years to make rocks such as carbonate (chalk).

Dead matter compacted in certain rock types is altered over millions of years to form fossil fuels.

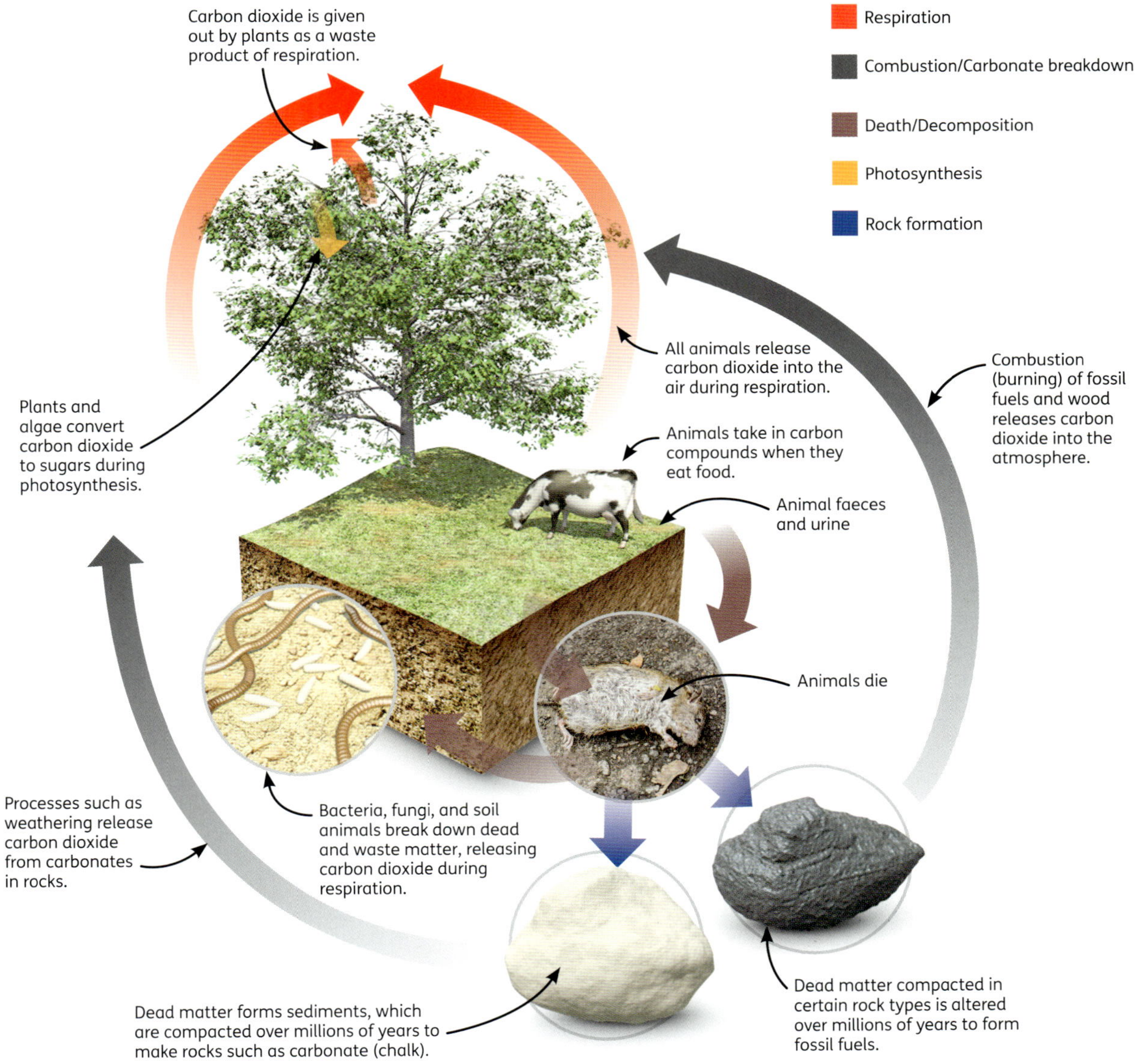

Human Impacts on Biodiversity

Key terms

- Biodiversity
- Deforestation
- Eutrophication
- Global warming
- Greenhouse gas
- Landfill site
- Peat
- Reforestation

Key facts

- Biodiversity is the variety of all the different species in an ecosystem.
- Biodiversity makes ecosystems stable by providing a variety of species for organisms to use for resources (for example food, shelter).
- Many human activities reduce biodiversity, but conservation measures are being introduced.
- With more humans and higher living standards, we increase global warming, need more land, need more food and so produce more waste. These all reduce biodiversity.

Some species cannot survive if their ecosystems become warmer. This reduces biodiversity. An example is in coral reefs. Corals are animals with algae living in them. The algae get protection and, in return, provide food for the coral. If the water warms up, the algae leave the coral.

Global warming

Global warming is the increase in average temperatures around the world. It is caused by increases in **greenhouse gases** in the atmosphere, which trap heat. These are released by:

- Electricity generation: burning fossil fuels in power stations releases CO_2.
- Transport: burning fossil fuels in engines releases CO_2.
- Food production: fossil fuels power machinery. Rice fields release methane.
- **Deforestation** and burning **peat** release CO_2.

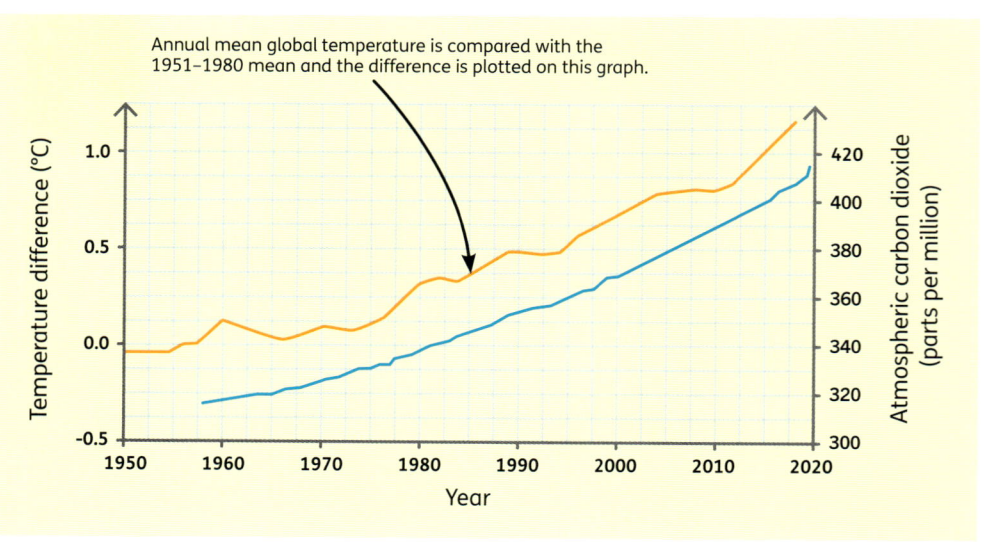

This graph shows that atmospheric carbon dioxide and mean global temperature have both increased over the last 50 years. If atmospheric carbon dioxide continues to rise, then global warming is likely to continue.

Annual mean global temperature is compared with the 1951–1980 mean and the difference is plotted on this graph.

Ecology

> **Land use**
>
> Land use reduces biodiversity. We use land for:
>
> - Building.
> - Dumping waste (**landfill sites**).
> - Farming.
> - Extracting resources (for example stone, peat).
>
> Peat is partially decomposed plant material. It is removed from peat bogs for garden compost. Without peat, other bog organisms die.

Farming

Burning down forests to create farmland releases CO_2, and results in fewer trees to use up CO_2.

Tropical forests have been destroyed for land to grow rice and biofuels and keep cattle.

Farm animals and their diseases can escape into new areas and wipe out other species.

Waste and pollution

Toxic substances from factory waste can pollute air, water and land. They poison organisms. Toxic substances often leak into the soil from landfill sites.

Fish farming reduces water quality due to waste produced by fish.

When sewage or fertilisers from farms enter water, it causes nutrient overload (**eutrophication**).

Eutrophication

Maintaining biodiversity

We can maintain biodiversity by:

- Having breeding programmes for **endangered** species to stop them from becoming **extinct**.
- Reducing deforestation.
- Protecting and regenerating habitats (including **reforestation**).
- Preserving hedges and saving parts of farms for wild plants, not crops.
- Reducing CO_2 emissions by using **renewable** energy.
- **Recycling** resources to reduce landfill.

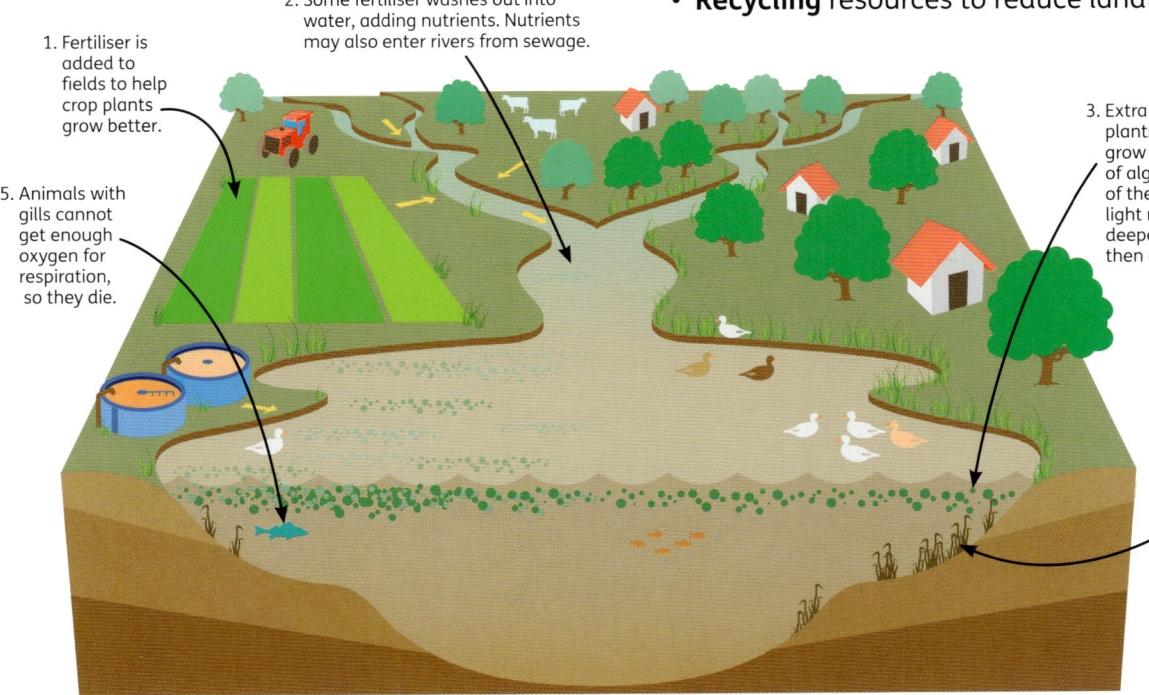

1. Fertiliser is added to fields to help crop plants grow better.
2. Some fertiliser washes out into water, adding nutrients. Nutrients may also enter rivers from sewage.
3. Extra nutrients cause plants and algae to grow faster. The growth of algae on the surface of the water prevents light reaching plants deeper down, which then die.
4. Decaying plants stimulate the growth of decomposers, such as bacteria. They use up oxygen in the water.
5. Animals with gills cannot get enough oxygen for respiration, so they die.

Food Security

Key terms

- Biotechnology
- Fermenter
- Food security
- Fusarium
- Genetic engineering
- Genetically modified organism (GMO)
- Mycoprotein
- Overfishing
- Quota
- Sustainable
- Yield

Reducing food security

Food security is having enough food to feed a population. It is being reduced by:

- Increasing birth rates – more people demand more food.
- New pests and diseases reduce crop **yields** and livestock health.
- Pollution can kill plants and livestock.
- Climate change – global warming is changing weather patterns, causing more flooding and droughts.
- Increasing costs – more expensive livestock, seeds, fertilisers and pesticides reduce food supply.
- Conflicts – wars and unstable governments limit access to food and water.
- Biofuels reduce the land available for growing food crops.
- Changing diets in developed countries reduce food supply elsewhere due to increased demand for:
  - New and unusual foods from less developed countries.
  - Meat (rearing livestock reduces the land area for local crops).

Increasing food security

Food security can be increased by:

- Using sustainable farming methods. This means doing things in ways that maintain resources, so they can continue to meet demand in the future.
- Farming more efficiently. Farmers can use high-protein feeds to increase animal growth. Animals will also waste less energy if kept warm and stopped from moving too much.
- Encourage people to eat less meat. Less energy, land and water are needed for food crops compared with livestock.

Food crops produce less greenhouse gas

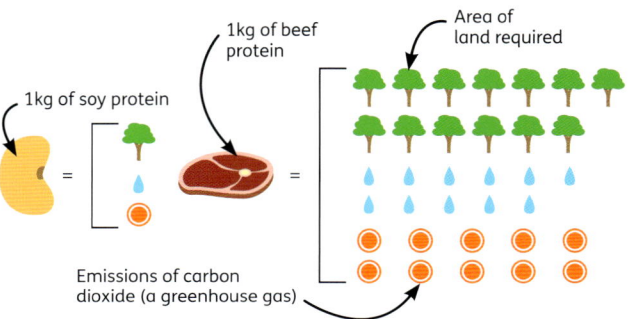

Overfishing

Overfishing is taking so many fish from seas that populations fall.

Sustainable fishing methods catch fewer fish. This lets more fish reproduce, and so populations are maintained. This is done by:

- Using **quotas** – limits on how many fish can be caught.
- Increasing net mesh size – larger holes in nets allow more young fish to escape and breed.
- Farming fish reduces the number of wild fish taken from the seas.
- Creating marine reserves where fishing is not allowed.
- Reducing consumption of some fish and encouraging people to eat seafood from sustainable sources.

Ecology 107

Key facts

Biotechnology is using living things to do specific tasks or make valuable substances. Examples include bread-making, growing crops for biofuels and growing large quantities of microorganisms for food.

Genetic engineering

A genetically engineered or genetically modified organism (GMO) has had its DNA altered by scientists (see pages 94–95).

- GM bacteria produce human **insulin** for diabetes treatment.
- GM crops provide more food because they grow faster or are **resistant** to diseases.
- GM crops provide food with specific nutrients.

Mycoprotein

Fusarium is a fungus that can be grown on glucose syrup in aerobic conditions to produce a food for humans called **mycoprotein**. It is rich in proteins and suitable for vegetarians. It is made in huge **fermenters**.

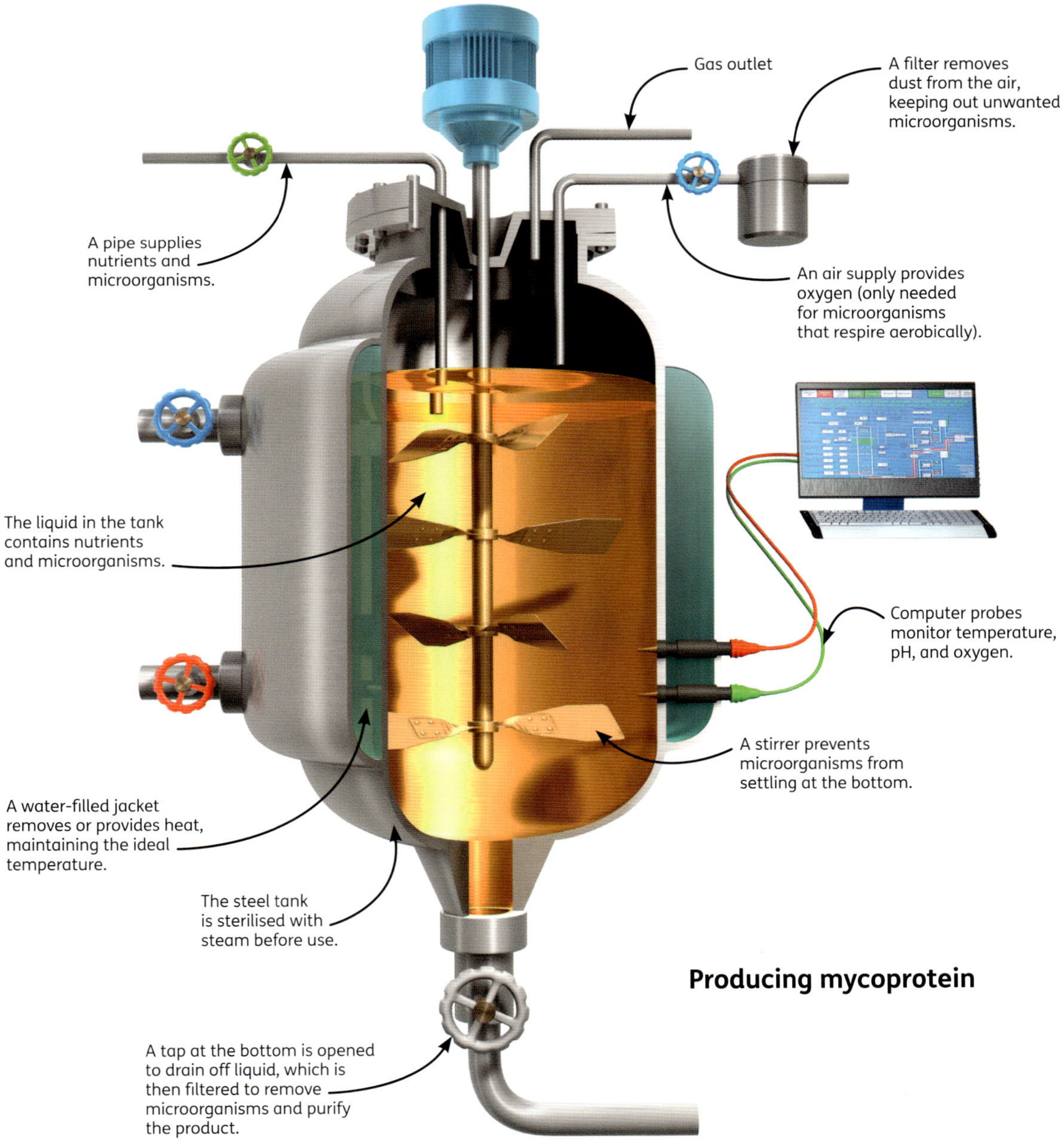

- Gas outlet
- A filter removes dust from the air, keeping out unwanted microorganisms.
- A pipe supplies nutrients and microorganisms.
- An air supply provides oxygen (only needed for microorganisms that respire aerobically).
- The liquid in the tank contains nutrients and microorganisms.
- Computer probes monitor temperature, pH, and oxygen.
- A stirrer prevents microorganisms from settling at the bottom.
- A water-filled jacket removes or provides heat, maintaining the ideal temperature.
- The steel tank is sterilised with steam before use.
- A tap at the bottom is opened to drain off liquid, which is then filtered to remove microorganisms and purify the product.

Producing mycoprotein

Ecology Recap Quiz

Find a pen and paper and work through these revision questions.

1. Complete the sentences. Each blank is one word.
   The number of individuals of a species is its _____ . All the species in an ecosystem are a _____ .

2. Look at this food chain.   grass → grasshopper → lizard → hawk
   There are 75 tonnes of primary consumers and 33 tonnes of secondary consumers. Calculate the efficiency of biomass transfer. Give your answer as a decimal or percentage.

3. Which of these are abiotic factors? Select all that apply.
   rainfall   soil pH   foxes   oak trees   eagles   bacteria

4. The table shows some results from quadrat sampling in a field.
   Estimate the daisy plant population. Each quadrat was a square measuring 1 m × 1 m. The field was 1500 m².

Quadrat number	1	2	3	4	5	6	7	8	9	10	11	12
Number of daisy plants	2	0	2	4	9	8	3	2	8	0	1	3

5. Which one of the following is a gas produced by aerobic respiration of bacteria?
   sulfur dioxide   oxygen   nitrogen dioxide   carbon dioxide

6. What do decomposers secrete that allows them to feed?
   hormones   enzymes   carbon dioxide   glucose

7. Which of these conditions speeds up making compost from kitchen scraps? Choose one.
   warmer temperatures   less oxygen
   less water   anaerobic conditions

8. Give the reason why stopping farm animals from moving too much will allow them to grow faster.

Check your answers on page **109**.

Answers

Cell Biology — 18

1. Osmosis, partially/semi-
2. Plasmid(s)
3. Neurone / neuron / nerve cell
4. One of: repair, asexual reproduction, growth/development of multicellular organisms
5. • increases the rate • because particles move faster
6. area of one side = 6.25 cm², so area of six sides is 6 × 6.25 = 37.5 cm². Volume = 15.625 cm³. SA:V = 0.4
7. resolution
8. Two of: organelles doubled, ribosomes doubled, DNA replicated/copied/doubled
9. xylem
10. Mineral(s) / mineral ion(s) / or any named mineral ion
11. To sterilise /prevent contamination
12. ×100
13. Adult stem cells can only produce a limited range of specialised cells
14. Chloroplast
15. To prevent condensation dripping onto cultures

Organisation — 38

1. brain, kidney
2. It's a group of different cells working together to perform a function.
3. Biuret's solution
4. a) Carbohydrases break down carbohydrates into simple sugars.
   b) Proteases break down proteins into amino acids.
   c) Lipases break down lipids (fats) into glycerol and fatty acids.
5. Any one from: emulsifies fats / (is alkaline so) neutralises hydrochloric acid
6. Its active site is a specific shape, which is complementary to/only fits with its substrate
7. a) Thick muscle and elastic walls, small lumen
   b) Thin muscle and elastic walls, large lumen, valves
   c) Very thin permeable walls (one cell thick)
8. Any four from: statins, stents, mechanical/physical valves, heart transplant, artificial heart
9. Uncontrolled cell division
10. Palisade mesophyll
11. Transport of dissolved sugars around a plant (in the phloem)
12. Temperature, humidity, light intensity, wind speed

Infection and Response — 50

1. Pathogen
2. Malaria
3. Lymphocytes
4. Mosquito
5. Kills bacteria
6. Magnesium
7. • antigens from/weakened/inactive/dead pathogen
   • causes memory cells
   • (ready to) release antibodies (in large amounts and quickly) when pathogen is met
8. Barrier to microorganisms/pathogens
   • falls off taking microorganisms/pathogens with it
9. Clinial trial
10. • droplets from coughs/sneezes • in the air
11. Antibiotics
12. • phagocyte • surrounds micoorganism/pathogen
    • engulfs/digests/destroys it
13. Antiviral
14. One of: fever, abdominal cramps, vomiting, diarrhoea

Bioenergetics — 58

1. Mitochondria
2. Any two from: for energy (respiration), to make cellulose / amino acids / fats and oils / sucrose
3. Water + carbon dioxide → glucose + oxygen
4. $C_6H_{12}O_6$
5. Count the number of bubbes of oxygen produced/volume of oxygen produced (collected in a gas syringe).
6. a) 35°C
   b) Reaction will occur slowly at 20°C as the particles are not moving very fast, but at 50°C the enzymes involved in photosynthesis will be denatured so photosynthesis will stop.
7. More efficient / more energy transferred per glucose molecule and it does not produce lactic acid.

Answers

8. The breathing rate increases to take in more oxygen (and remove more carbon dioxide). The heart beats faster to pump blood around the body quicker, delivering more oxygen to the cells so they can respire.
9. Any one from: making beer / making bread / making wine or any other relevant example
10. Metabolism is the sum of all the reactions in a cell or the body.

Homeostasis and Response   78

1. Rain
2. Insulin
3. Neurones
4. a) receptor b) coordinator c) effector
5. Retina
6. a) LH / luteinising hormone
   b) FSH / follicle stimulating hormone
7. a) • growth (of a plant • away from • light
   b) • in roots • auxin • moves away from light / to shady parts •inhibits growth/elongation
8. Two from: water, blood sugar, temperature nitrogen,
9. • sensory neurone • relay neurone • motor neurone
10. Gets thinner
11. • sweat • vasodilation/widening of blood vessels (in the dermis)
12. Urea

Inheritance, Variation and Evolution   96

1. asexual
2. strawberry   daffodil
3. Mitosis (there are two types of cell division, so you need to be specific)
4. Meiosis (difficult to spell … but the three vowels "eio" are in alphabetical order)
5. Sugar / ribose • phoshate group • base
6. One of: implies that people with inherited disorders are inferior OR makes people want to have designer / perfect babies OR expensive for the health service
7. Polydactyly is the expected answer but there are others (for example Achondroplasia, Huntington's disease, Marfan's syndrome • neurofibromatosis, Von Willebrand's disease)
8. One of: it did not include a divine creator/god, it could not explain how variation occurred, it could not explain how characteristics were inherited, fossils at the time show that evolution was not gradual – there were sudden jumps.
9. (during fossilisation) the bones are replaced by minerals
10. One of: • resistant to disease/insect attack • which increases yield, • produces a certain substance • that is valuable/useful, • better yields/ more growth • more profit. (In an "explain" question you will need to make at least two points. Here you need to say what is done and why it is done.)

Ecology   108

1. a) population   b) community
2. 0.44 or 44%
3. rainfall   soil pH
4. 42/12 = 3.5. plants/m2, 3.5 × 1500 = 5,250
5. carbon dioxide
6. enzymes
7. warmer temperatures
8. Animals waste/use/lose less energy

Exam Board References

Pages	AQA	Edexcel
6–7	4.1.1.1, 4.1.1.2, 4.1.1.5	1.1, 1.3, 1.4, 1.5, 1.6
8–9	4.1.1.1, 4.1.1.6	1.1, 5.17B, 5.18B, 5.19B
10–11	4.1.2.1, 4.1.2.2, 4.1.1.4	2.1, 2.2, 2.3, 2.5, 2.6
12–13	4.1.2.3, 4.1.1.3	1.2, 2.8, 2.9, 6.7
14–15	4.1.3.1, 4.1.3.2, 4.1.3.3	1.15, 1.16, 1.17
16–17	4.1.3.1	8.1, 8.2, 8.3, 8.4B
20–21	4.2.1, 4.2.2.1, 4.2.2.3	8.6
22–23	4.2.2.1	1.13B
24–25	4.2.2.1	1.44–1.46, 1.49
26–27	4.2.2.1	1.7, 1.8, 1.9, 1.10, 1.11
28–29	4.2.2.2	8.7, 8.8
30–31	4.2.2.2, 4.2.2.4	8.8, 8.12
32–33	4.2.2.5, 4.2.2.6, 4.2.2.7	2.4, 5.23, 5.24, 5.25
34–35	4.2.3.1, 4.2.3.2	6.8, 6.9, 6.10, 6.11B
36–37	4.2.3.2	6.12, 6.13
40–41	4.3.1.1, 4.3.1.2, 4.3.1.3, 4.3.1.4, 4.3.1.5	5.2, 5.4, 5.5, 5.6, 5.8
42–43	4.3.1.1, 4.3.1.2	5.4, 5.5, 5.6, 5.7B, 5.8
44–45	4.3.1.1, 4.3.1.6, 4.3.1.7	5.12, 5.13, 5.14, 5.15B
46–47	4.3.1.8, 4.3.1.9	5.16, 5.17B, 5.18B, 5.19B, 5.20
48–49	4.3.3.1, 4.3.3.2	5.5, 5.6, 5.9B, 5.10B
52–53	4.4.1.1, 4.4.1.3, 4.4.2.3	6.2
54–55	4.4.1.2	6.3, 6.5
56–57	4.4.2.1, 4.4.2.2, 4.4.2.3	8.9. 8.10
60–61	4.5.1, 4.5.2.1	2.13, 2.14, 7.9
62–63	4.5.2.2, 4.5.2.4	2.10B, 7.10B, 7.11B, 7.12B
64–65	4.5.2.3	2.15B, 2.16B, 2.17B
66–67	4.5.3.1	7.1
68–69	4.5.3.2	7.13, 7.15, 7.16, 7.17
70–71	4.5.3.3	7.18B, 7.19B, 7.21B, 7.22B
72–73	4.5.3.4	7.4
74–75	4.5.3.5	7.5, 7.7
76–77	4.5.4, 4.5.4.1	6.15B
80–81	4.6.1.1, 4.6.1.2, 4.6.1.3	3.1B, 3.2B, 3.3, 3.20
82–83	4.6.1.4, 4.6.1.5	3.4, 3.5, 3.6, 3.21
84–85	4.6.1.6	3.12, 3.13, 3.14, 3.16, 3.19
86–87	4.6.1.6, 4.6.1.7, 4.6.1.8, 4.6.3.3	3.11B, 3.14, 3.15, 3.17B
88–89	4.6.2.1, 4.6.2.3, 4.6.4	3.23, 4.7, 4.8
90–91	4.6.2.1, 4.6.2.2, 4.6.3.1, 4.6.3.2	3.22, 4.1B, 4.2
92–93	4.6.3.4, 4.6.3.5, 4.6.3.6, 4.6.3.7	4.3, 4.4, 4.5
94–95	4.6.2.4, 4.6.2.5	4.9B, 4.10, 4.11, 4.12B, 4.14
98–99	4.7.1.1, 4.7.1.2, 4.7.1.3, 4.7.1.4	6.14B, 9.1, 9.2, 9.3, 9.4
100–101	4.7.2.1, 4.7.4.1, 4.7.4.2, 4.7.4.3	6.1, 9.5, 9.6, 9.7B, 9.8B
102–103	4.7.2.2, 4.7.2.3	9.12, 9.13, 9.14, 9.15, 9.17B, 9.18B, 9.19B
104–105	4.7.3.2, 4.7.3.3, 4.7.3.4, 4.7.3.5, 4.7.3.6	9.9, 9.10
106–107	4.7.5.1, 4.7.5.2, 4.7.5.3, 4.7.5.4	9.11B

Acknowledgments

The publisher would like to thank the following for their kind permission to reproduce their photographs:

(Key: a-above; b-below/bottom; c-centre; f-far; l-left; r-right; t-top)

7 Dreamstime.com: Elena Schweitzer / Egal (bl). **9 Dreamstime.com:** Ggw1962 (bl). **11 Getty Images / iStock:** ELyrae (br). **14 Adobe Stock:** Tasha Vector (br). **Shutterstock.com:** petrroudny43 (bl). **15 Science Photo Library:** (cr). **17 Science Photo Library:** EYE OF SCIENCE (c). **Shutterstock.com:** Tatsiana M (tr). **28 Alamy Stock Photo:** Aldona Griskeviciene (crb/x3). **Shutterstock.com:** Amadeu Blasco (br/x3). **31 Dreamstime.com:** Glolyla (clb/x2). **33 Science Photo Library:** Steve Gschmeissner (bc). **36 Alamy Stock Photo:** Scenics & Science (br). **Science Photo Library:** Dr Jeremy Burgess (cl); Eye Of Science (cr); Steve Gschmeissner (bl). **40 Alamy Stock Photo:** Alexey Kotelnikov (bc). **42 Dreamstime.com:** Skypixel (bl). **43 123RF.com:** gl0ck33 (tr). **45 Getty Images:** AFP / Narinder Nanu / Stringer (bl). **46 Science Photo Library:** CNRI (br). **47 Dreamstime.com:** Ahmad Firdaus Ismail (br); Jenifoto406 (cr). **48 Adobe Stock:** Martina (cla). **Alamy Stock Photo:** Yon Marsh Natural History (cl). **Shutterstock.com:** Plant Pathology (clb). **49 Alamy Stock Photo:** Nature Picture Library / Adrian Davies (bl); Steve Tulley (cr). **Dreamstime.com:** Multik (br). **Shutterstock.com:** Pee Paew (c). **52 Getty Images / iStock:** E+ / Andy445 (bl). **Science Photo Library:** John Durham (cr). **53 Dreamstime.com:** Ksushsh (cb). **67 Alamy Stock Photo:** Connect Images / Herbert Spichtinger (cla). **80 Science Photo Library:** London School Of Hygiene & Tropical Medicine (cra). **84-85 Dorling Kindersley:** Wildlife Heritage Foundation, Kent, UK (leopard). **86 Alamy Stock Photo:** Juan Gartner / Science Photo Library (b). **88 Science Photo Library:** Geoff Kidd (bc). **91 Alamy Stock Photo:** FineArt (bl); GL Archive (bc). **94 Shutterstock.com:** Julee Ashmead (c). **95 Dreamstime.com:** Isselee (cb). **Science Photo Library:** Rosenfeld Images Ltd (cra). **98 Dreamstime.com:** Christian Edelmann (bl). **Getty Images / iStock:** E+ / ugurhan (cb); Robby_Holmwood (crb); E+ / CasarsaGuru (br). **101 Dorling Kindersley:** Stephen Oliver (cr). **103 123RF.com:** sunnytoys (cb)

Cover images: Front and Back: **Adobe Stock:** miloje (Textured Background); Back: **Dreamstime.com:** Beaniebeagle clb/ (Tubes), Vladimir Gladcov clb, Sergey Kolesov clb/ (Mark), Mex D clb/ (brain), Ylivdesign clb/ (explosion)

About the author

Matt Green, aka The Rapping Science Teacher, is a TikTok sensation, TV broadcaster, author and business owner, famous for his viral rapping science videos across social media.

Thanks to Matt's educational and entertaining videos and his performances of acclaimed freestyles on TV and radio, Matt, the former Head of Chemistry at a London comprehensive school, now has millions of followers across his social media platforms and is a regular guest on primetime TV and radio shows.

Content creator Matt works with many leading brands, and uses his teaching skills to educate and entertain students on social media by releasing 30-second GCSE science rap videos every week, with subjects ranging from respiration to electrolysis, teamed with chart-topping soundtracks.

Matt now brings you three new revision guides with his famous TikTok raps to help you to **Rap. Revise. Remember!**